THE BURIED TEMPLE

I0682274

MAURICE MAETERLINCK

Translated by Alfred Sutro

The Buried Temple

Maurice Maeterlinck

© 1st World Library, 2009
PO Box 2211
Fairfield, IA 52556
www.1stworldlibrary.com
First Edition

LCCN: 2009923474

Softcover ISBN: 978-1-4218-8865-1
Hardcover ISBN: 978-1-4218-8964-1
eBook ISBN: 978-1-4218-8766-1

Purchase *"The Buried Temple"*
as a traditional bound book at:
www.1stWorldLibrary.com/purchase.asp?ISBN=978-1-4218-8865-1

1st World Library is a literary, educational organization
dedicated to:

- Creating a free internet library of downloadable ebooks

- Hosting writing competitions and offering book publishing
scholarships.

Interested in more 1st World Library books? contact:
literacy@1stworldlibrary.com
Check us out at: www.1stworldlibrary.com

1ˢᵗ World Library Literary Society

Giving Back to the World

"If you want to work on the core problem, it's early school literacy."

- James Barksdale, former CEO of Netscape

"No skill is more crucial to the future of a child, or to a democratic and prosperous society, than literacy."

- Los Angeles Times

"Literacy... means far more than learning how to read and write... The aim is to transmit... knowledge and promote social participation."

- UNESCO

"Literacy is not a luxury, it is a right and a responsibility. If our world is to meet the challenges of the twenty-first century we must harness the energy and creativity of all our citizens."

- President Bill Clinton

"Parents should be encouraged to read to their children, and teachers should be equipped with all available techniques for teaching literacy, so the varying needs and capacities of individual kids can be taken into account."

- Hugh Mackay

NOTE

Of the five essays in this volume, two only, those on "The Past" and "Luck," were written in 1901. The others, "The Mystery of Justice," "The Evolution of Mystery," and "The Kingdom of Matter," are anterior to "The Life of the Bee," and appeared in the *Fortnightly Review* in 1899 and 1900. The essay on "The Past" appeared in the March number of the *Fortnightly Review* and of the New York *Independent*; and parts of "The Mystery of Justice" in this last journal and *Harper's Magazine*. The author's thanks are due to Messrs. Chapman & Hall, Messrs. Harper & Brothers, and the proprietors of *The Independent* for their permission to republish.

CONTENTS

I

THE MYSTERY OF JUSTICE

1

I speak, for those who do not believe in the existence of a unique, all-powerful, infallible Judge, for ever intent on our thoughts, our feelings and actions, maintaining justice in this world and completing it in the next. And if there be no Judge, what justice is there? None other than that which men have made for themselves by their laws and tribunals, as also in the social relations that no definite judgment governs? Is there nothing above this human justice, whose sanction is rarely other than the opinion, the confidence or mistrust, the approval or disapproval, of our fellows? Is this capable of explaining or accounting for all that seems so inexplicable to us in the morality of the universe, that we at times feel almost compelled to believe an intelligent Judge must exist? When we deceive or overcome our neighbour, have we deceived or overcome all the forces of justice? Are all things definitely settled then, and may we go boldly on: or is there a graver, deeper justice, one less visible perhaps, but less subject to error; one that is more universal, and mightier?

That such a justice exists we all of us know, for we all have felt its irresistible power. We are well aware that it covers the whole of our life, and that at its centre there reigns an intelligence which never deceives itself, which none can deceive. But where shall we place it, now that we have torn it down from the skies? Where does it weigh good and evil, happiness and disaster? Whence does it issue to deal out reward and punishment? These are questions that we do not often ask ourselves, but they have their importance. The nature of justice, and all our morality, depend on the answer; and it cannot be fruitless therefore to inquire how that great idea of mystic and sovereign justice, which has undergone more than one transformation since history began, is being received to-day in the mind and the heart of man. And is this mystery not the loftiest, the most passionately interesting, of all that remain to us: does it not intertwine with most of the others? Do its vacillations not stir us to the very depths of our soul? The great bulk of mankind perhaps know nothing of these vacillations and changes, but for the evolution of thought it suffices that the eyes of the few should see; and when the clear consciousness of these has become aware of the transformation, its influence will gradually attain the general morality of men.

2

In these pages we shall naturally have much to say of social justice: of the justice, in other words, that we mutually extend to each other through life; but we shall leave on one side legal or positive justice, which is merely the organisation of one side of social justice. We shall occupy ourselves above all with that vague but inevitable justice, intangible and yet so effective, which accompanies and sets its seal upon every action of our life; which approves or disapproves, rewards or punishes. Does this come from without? Does an inflexible, undeceivable moral principle exist, independent of man, in the universe and in things? Is there, in a word, a justice that might be called mystic? Or does it issue wholly from man; is it inward even though it act from without; and is the only justice therefore psychologic? These two terms, mystic and psychologic justice, comprehend, more or less, all the different forms of justice, superior to the social, that would appear to exist to-day.

3

It is scarcely conceivable that any one who has forsaken the easy, but artificially illumined, paths of positive religion, can still believe in the existence of a physical justice arising from moral causes, whether its manifestations assume the form of heredity or disease, of geologic, atmospheric, or other phenomena. However eager his desire for illusion or mystery, this is a truth he is bound to recognise from the moment he begins earnestly and sincerely to study his own personal experience, or to observe the external ills which, in this world of ours, fall indiscriminately on good and wicked alike. Neither the earth nor the sky, neither nature nor matter, neither air nor any force known to man (save only those that are in him) betrays the slightest regard for justice, or the remotest connection with our morality, our thoughts or intentions. Between the external world and our actions there exist only the simple and essentially non-moral relations of cause and effect. If I am guilty of a certain excess or imprudence, I incur a certain danger, and have to pay a corresponding debt to nature. And as this imprudence or excess will generally have had an immoral cause—or a cause that we call immoral because we have been compelled to regulate our life according to the requirements of our health and tranquillity—we cannot refrain from establishing a connection between this immoral cause and the danger to which we have been exposed, or the debt we have had to pay; and we are led once more to believe in the justice of the universe, the prejudice which, of all those that we cling to, has its root deepest in our heart. And in our eagerness to restore this confidence we are content deliberately to ignore the fact that the result would have been exactly the same had the cause of our excess or imprudence been—to use the terms of our infantine vocabulary—heroic or innocent. If on an intensely cold day I throw myself into the water to save a fellow-creature from drowning, or if, seeking to drown him, I chance to fall in, the consequences of the chill will be absolutely the same; and nothing on this earth or beneath the sky—save only myself, or man if he be able—will enhance my suffering because I have committed a crime, or relieve my pain because my action was virtuous.

4

Let us consider another form of physical justice: heredity. There again we find the same indifference to moral causes. And truly it were a strange justice indeed that would throw upon the son, and even the remote descendant, the burden of a fault committed by his father or his ancestor. But human morality would raise no objection: man would not protest. To him it would seem natural, magnificent, even fascinating. It would indefinitely prolong his individuality, his conscious-ness and existence; and from this point of view would accord with a number of indisputable facts which prove that we are not wholly self-contained, but connect, in more than one subtle, mysterious fashion, with all that surrounds us in life, with all that precedes us, or follows.

And yet, true as this may be in certain cases, it is not true as regards the justice of physical heredity, which is absolutely indifferent to the moral causes of the deed whose cones-quences the descendants have to bear. There is physical relation between the act of the father, whereby he has undermined his health, and the consequent suffering of the son; but the son's suffering will be the same whatever the intentions or motives of the father, be these heroic or shameful. And, further, the area of what we call the justice of physical heredity would appear to be very restricted. A father may have been guilty of a hundred abominable crimes, he may have been a murderer, a traitor, a persecutor of the innocent or despoiler of the wretched, without these crimes leaving the slightest trace upon the organism of his children. It is enough that he should have been careful to do nothing that might injure his health.

5

So much for the justice of Nature as shown in physical heredity. Moral heredity would appear to be governed by similar principles; but as it deals with modifications of the mind and character infinitely more complex and more elusive, its manifestations are less striking, and its results less certain. Pathology is the only region which admits of its definite observation and study; and there we observe it to be merely the spiritual form of physical heredity, which is its essential principle: moral heredity being only a sequel, and revealing in its elementary stage the same indifference to real justice, and the same blindness. Whatever the moral cause of the ancestor's drunkenness or debauch, the same punishment may be meted out in mind and body to the descendants of the drunkard or the debauchee. Intellectual blemish will almost always accompany material blemish. The soul will be attacked simultaneously with the body; and it matters but little whether the victim be imbecile, mad, epileptic, possessed of criminal instincts, or only vaguely threatened with slight mental derangement: the most frightful moral penalty that a supreme justice could invent has followed actions which, as a rule, cause less harm and are less perverse than hundreds of other offences that Nature never dreams of punishing. And this penalty, moreover, is inflicted blindly, not the slightest heed being paid to the motives underlying the actions, motives that may have been excusable perhaps, or indifferent, or possibly even admirable.

It would be absurd, however, to imagine that drunkenness and debauchery are the only agents in moral heredity. There are a thousand others, all more or less unknown. Certain moral qualities appear to be transmitted as readily as though they were physical. In one race, for instance, we will almost constantly discover certain virtues which have probably been acquired. But who shall say how much is due to heredity, and how much to environment and example? The problem becomes so complicated, the facts so contradictory, that it is impossible, amidst the mass of innumerable causes, to follow the track of one particular cause to the end. Let it suffice to say that in the only clear, striking, definitive cases where an intentional justice could have revealed itself in physical or moral heredity, no trace of justice is found. And if we do not find it in these, we are surely far less likely to find it in others.

6

We may affirm therefore that not above us, or around us, or beneath us, neither in this life nor in our other life which is that of our children, is the least trace to be found of an intentional justice. But, in the course of adapting ourselves to the laws of life, we have naturally been led to credit with our own moral ideas those principles of causality that we encounter most frequently; and we have in this fashion created a very plausible semblance of effective justice, which rewards or punishes most of our actions in the degree that they approach, or deviate from, certain laws that are essential for the preservation of the race. It is evident that if I sow my field, I shall have an infinitely better prospect of reaping a harvest the following summer than my neighbour, who has neglected to sow his, preferring a life of dissipation and idleness. In this case, therefore, work obtains its admirable and certain reward; and as work is essential for the preservation of our existence, we have declared it to be the moral act of all acts, the first of all our duties. Such instances might be indefinitely multiplied. If I bring up my children well, if I am good and just to those round about me, if I am honest, active, prudent, wise, and sincere in all my dealings, I shall have a better chance of meeting with filial piety, with respect and affection, a better chance of knowing moments of happiness, than the man whose actions and conduct have been the very reverse of mine. Let us not, however, lose sight of the fact that my neighbour, who is, let us say, a most diligent and thrifty man, might be prevented by the most admirable of reasons—such as an illness caught while nursing his wife or his friend—from sowing his ground at the proper time, and that he also would reap no harvest. *Mutatis mutandis*, similar results would follow in the other instances I have mentioned. The cases, however, are exceptional where a worthy or respectable reason will hinder the accomplishment of a duty; and we shall find, as a rule, that sufficient harmony exists between cause and effect, between the exaction of the necessary law and the result of the complying effort, to enable our casuistry to keep alive within us the idea of the justice of things.

7

This idea, however, deeply ingrained though it be in the hearts and minds of the least credulous and least mystic of men, can surely not be beneficial. It reduces our morality to the level of the insect which, perched on a falling rock, imagines that the rock has been set in motion on its own special behalf. Are we wise in allowing certain errors and falsehoods to remain active within us? There may have been some in the past which, for a moment, were helpful; but, this moment over, men found themselves once again face to face with the truth, and the sacrifice had only been delayed. Why wait till the illusion or falsehood which appeared to do good begins to do actual harm, or, if it do no harm, at least retards the perfect understanding that should obtain between the deeply felt reality and our manner of interpreting and accepting it? What were the divine right of kings, the infallibility of the Church, the belief in rewards beyond the grave, but illusions whose sacrifice reason deferred too long? Nor was anything gained by this dilatoriness beyond a few sterile hopes, a little deceptive peace, a few consolations that at times were disastrous. But many days had been lost; and we have no days to lose, we who at last are seeking the truth, and find in its search an all-sufficient reason for existence. Nor does anything retard us more than the illusion which, though torn from its roots, we still permit to linger among us; for this will display the most extraordinary activity and be constantly changing its form.

But what does it matter, some will ask, whether man do the thing that is just because he thinks God is watching; because he believes in a kind of justice that pervades the universe; or for the simple reason that to his conscience this thing seems just? It matters above all. We have there three different men. The first, whom God is watching, will do much that is not just, for every god whom man has hitherto worshipped has decreed many unjust things. And the second will not always act in the same way as the third, who is indeed the true man to whom the moralist will turn, for he will survive both the others; and to foretell how man will conduct himself in truth, which is his natural element, is more interesting to the moralist than to watch his behaviour when enmeshed in falsehood.

8

It may seem idle to those who do not believe in the existence
of a sovereign Judge to discuss so seriously this inadmissible
idea of the justice of things; and inadmissible it does indeed
become when presented thus in its true colours, as it were,
pinned to the wall. This, however, is not our way of
regarding it in every-day life. When we observe how disaster
follows crime, how ruin at last overtakes ill-gotten prosperity; when we witness the miserable end of the debauchee,
the short-lived triumph of iniquity, it is our constant habit to
confuse the physical effect with the moral cause; and
however little we may believe in the existence of a Judge, we
nearly all of us end by a more or less complete submission to
a strange, vague faith in the justice of things. And although
our reason, our calm observation, prove to us that this justice
cannot exist, it is enough that an event should take place
which touches us somewhat more nearly, or that there should
be two or three curious coincidences, for conviction to fade
in our heart, if not in our mind. Notwithstanding all our
reason and all our experience, the merest trifle recalls to life
within us the ancestor who was convinced that the stars
shone in their eternal places for no other purpose than to
predict or approve a wound he was to inflict on his enemy
upon the field of battle, a word he should speak in the
assembly of the chiefs, or an intrigue he would bring to a
successful issue in the women's quarters. We of to-day are no
less inclined to divinise our feelings for the benefit of our
interests; the only difference being that, the gods having no
longer a name, our methods are less sincere and less precise.
When the Greeks, powerless before Troy, felt the need of
supernatural signal and support, they went to Philoctetes,
deprived him of Hercules' bow and arrows, and abandoned

him, ill, naked, and defenceless, on a desert island. This was the mysterious Justice, loftier than that of man; this was the command of the gods. And similarly do we, when some iniquity seems expedient to us, cry loudly that we do it for the sake of posterity, of humanity, of the fatherland. On the other hand, should a great misfortune befall us, we protest that there is no justice, and that there are no gods; but let the misfortune befall our enemy, and the universe is at once repeopled with invisible judges. If, however, some unexpected, disproportionate stroke of good fortune come to us, we are quickly convinced that we must possess merits so carefully hidden as to have escaped our own observation; and we are happier in their discovery than at the windfall they have procured us.

9

"One has to pay for all things," we say. Yes, in the depths of our heart, in all that pertains to man, justice exacts payment in the coin of our personal happiness or sorrow. And without, in the universe that enfolds us, there is also a reckoning; but here it is a different paymaster who measures out happiness or sorrow. Other laws obtain; there are other motives, other methods. It is no longer the justice of the conscience that presides, but the logic of nature, which cares nothing for our morality. Within us is a spirit that weighs only intentions; without us, a power that only balances deeds. We try to persuade ourselves that these two work hand in hand. But in reality, though the spirit will often glance towards the power, this last is as completely ignorant of the other's existence as is the man weighing coals in Northern Europe of the existence of his fellow weighing diamonds in South Africa. We are constantly intruding our sense of justice into this non-moral logic; and herein lies the source of most of our errors.

And further, what right have we to complain of the indifference of the universe, what right to declare it incomprehensible, and monstrous? Why this surprise at an injustice in which we ourselves take so active a part? It is true that there is no trace of justice to be found in disease, accident, or most of the hazards of external life, which fall indiscriminately on the good and the wicked, the hero and traitor, the poisoner and sister of charity. But we are far too eager to include under the title "Justice of the Universe" many a flagrant act that is exclusively human, and infinitely more common and more destructive than disease, the hurricane, or fire. I do not allude to war; it might be urged that we attribute this rather to the will of the people or kings than to Nature. But poverty, for instance, which we still rank with irremediable ills such as shipwreck or plague; poverty, with all its crushing sorrows and transmitted degeneration—how often may this be ascribed to the injustice of the elements, and how often to the injustice of our social condition, which is the crowning injustice of man? Need we, at the sight of unmerited wretchedness, look to the skies for a reason, as though a flash of lightning had caused it? Need we seek an impenetrable, unfathomable judge? Is this region not our own; are we not here in the best explored, best known portion of our dominion; and is it not we who organise misery, we who spread it abroad, as arbitrarily, from the moral point of view, as fire and disease scatter destruction or suffering? Is it reasonable that we should wonder at the sea's indifference to the soul-state of its victims, when we who have a soul, the pre-eminent organ of justice, pay no heed whatever to the innocence of the countless thousands whom we ourselves sacrifice, who are our wretched victims? We choose to regard as beyond our control, as a force of fatality, a force that rests entirely within our own hands. But does this excuse us? Truly we are strange lovers of an ideal justice, we are strange judges! A judicial error sends a thrill of horror from one end of the world to another; but the error which condemns three-fourths of mankind to misery, an error as purely human as that of any tribunal, is attributed by us to some inaccessible, implacable power. If the child of some honest man we know be born blind, imbecile, or deformed, we will seek everywhere, even in the darkness of a religion we have ceased to practise, for some God whose intention to question; but if the child be born poor—a calamity, as a rule, no less capable than the gravest infirmity of degrading a creature's destiny—we do not dream of interrogating the God who is wherever we are, since he is made of our own desires. Before we demand an ideal judge, we shall do well to purify our ideas, for whatever blemish there is in these will surely be in the judge. Before we complain of Nature's indifference, or ask at her hands an equity she does not possess, let us attack the iniquity that dwells in the homes of men; and when this has been swept away, we shall find that the part we assign to the injustice of fate will be less by fully two-thirds. And the benefit to mankind would be far more considerable than if it lay in our power to guide the storm or govern the heat and the cold, to direct the course of disease or the avalanche, or contrive that the sea should display an intelligent regard to our virtues and secret intentions. For indeed the poor far exceed in number those who fall victims to shipwreck or material accident, just as far more disease is due to material wretchedness than to the caprice of our organism, or to the hostility of the elements.

11

And for all that, we love justice. We live, it is true, in the midst of a great injustice; but we have only recently acquired this knowledge, and we still grope for a remedy. Injustice dates such a long way back; the idea of God, of destiny, of

Nature's mysterious decrees, had been so closely and intimately associated with it, it is still so deeply entangled with most of the unjust forces of the universe, that it was but yesterday that we commenced the endeavour to isolate such elements contained within it as are purely human. And if we succeed; if we can distinguish them, and separate them for all time from those upon which we have no power, justice will gain more than by all that the researches of man have discovered hitherto. For indeed in this social injustice of ours, it is not the human part that is capable of arresting our passion for equity; it is the part that a great number of men still attribute to a god, to a kind of fatality, or to imaginary laws of Nature.

12

This last inactive part shrinks every day. Nor is this because the mystery of justice is about to disappear. A mystery rarely disappears; as a rule, it only shifts its ground. But it is often most important and most desirable that we should bring about this change of abode. It may be said that two or three such changes almost stand for the whole progress of human thought: the dislodgment of two or three mysteries from a place where they did harm, and their transference to a place where they become inoffensive and capable of doing good. Sometimes even, there is no need for the mystery to change its place; we have only to identify it under another name. What was once called "the gods," we now term "life." And if life be as inexplicable as were the gods, we are at least the gainers to the extent that none has the right to speak or do wrong in its name. The aim of human thought can scarcely be to destroy mystery, or lessen it, for that seems impossible. We may be sure that the same quantity of mystery will ever enwrap the world, since it is the quality of the world, as of mystery, to be infinite. But honest human thought will seek above all to determine what are the veritable irreducible mysteries. It will endeavour to strip them of all that does not belong to them, that is not truly theirs, of the additions made by our errors, our fears, and our falsehoods. And as the artificial mysteries vanish, so will the ocean of veritable mystery stretch out further and further: the mystery of life, its aim and its origin; the mystery of thought; the mystery that has been called "the primitive accident," or the "perhaps unknowable essence of reality."

13

Where had men conceived the mystery of justice to lodge? It pervaded the world. At one moment it was supposed to rest in the hands of the gods, at another it engulfed and mastered the gods themselves. It had been imagined everywhere except in man. It had dwelt in the sky, it had lurked behind rocks, it had governed the air and the sea, it had peopled an inaccessible universe. Then at last we peered into its imaginary retreats, we pressed close and examined; and its throne of clouds tottered, it faded away; but at the very moment we believed it had ceased to be, behold it reappeared, and raised its head once more in the very depths of our heart; and yet another mystery had sought refuge in man, and embodied itself in him. For it is in ourselves that the mysteries we seek to destroy almost invariably find their last shelter and their most fitting abode, the home which they had forsaken, in the wildness of youth, to voyage through space; as it is in ourselves that we must learn to meet and to question them. And truly it is no less wonderful, no less inexplicable, that man should have in his heart an immutable instinct of justice, than it was wonderful and inexplicable that the gods should be just, or the forces of the universe. It is as difficult to account for the essence of our memory, our will, or intelligence, as it was to account for the memory, will, or intelligence of the invisible powers or laws of Nature; and if, in order to enhance our curiosity, we have need of the unknown or unknowable; if, in order to maintain our ardour, we require mystery or the infinite, we shall not lose a single tributary of the unknown and unknowable by at last restoring the great river to its primitive bed; nor shall we have closed a single road that leads to the infinite, or lessened by the minutest fraction the most contested of veritable mysteries. Whatever we take from the skies we find again in the heart of man. But, mystery for mystery, let us prefer the one that is certain to the one that is doubtful, the one that is near to the one that is far, the one that is in us and of us to the harmful one from without. Mystery for mystery, let us no longer parley with the messengers, but with the sovereign who sent them; no longer question those feeble ones who silently vanish at our first inquiry, but rather look into our heart, where are both question and answer; the answer which it has forgotten, but, some day perhaps, shall remember.

14

Then we shall be able to solve more than one disconcerting problem as to the distribution, often very equitable, of reward and punishment among men. And by this we do not mean only the inward, moral reward and punishment, but also the reward and punishment that are visible and wholly material. There was some measure of reason in the belief held by mankind from its very origin, that justice penetrates, animates as it were, every object of this world in which we live. This belief has not been explained away by the fact that our great moral laws have been forcibly adapted to the great laws of life and matter. There is more beyond. We cannot refer all things, in all circumstances, to a simple relation of cause and effect between crime and punishment. There is often a moral element also; and though events have not placed it there, though it is we alone who have created it, it is not the less powerful and real. Of a physical justice, properly so called, we deny the existence; but besides the wholly inward psychologic justice, to which we shall soon refer, there is also a psychologic justice which is in constant communication with the physical world; and it is this justice that we attribute to we know not what invisible and universal principle. And while it is wrong to credit Nature with moral intentions, and to allow our actions to be governed by fear of punishment or hope of reward that she may have in store for us, this does not imply that, even materially, there is no reward for good, or punishment for evil. Such reward and punishment undoubtedly exist, but they issue not from whence we imagine; and in believing that they come from an inaccessible spot, that they master us, judge us, and conesquently dispense us from judging ourselves, we commit the most dangerous of errors; for none has a greater influence upon our manner of defending ourselves against misfortune, or of setting forth to attempt the legitimate conquest of happiness.

15

Such justice as we actually discover in Nature does not issue from her, but from ourselves, who have unconsciously placed it there, through becoming one with events, animating them and adapting them to our uses. Accident, disease, the thunderbolt, which strike to right or to left, without apparent reason or warning, wholly indifferent as to what our thoughts may be, are not the only elements in our life. There are other, and far more frequent, cases when we have direct influence on the things and persons around us, and invest these with our own personality; cases when the forces of nature become the instruments of our thoughts, which, when unjust, will make improper use of them, thereby calling forth retaliation and inviting punishment and disaster. But in Nature there is no moral reaction; for this emanates from our own thoughts or the thoughts of other men. It is not in things, but in us, that the justice of things resides. It is our moral condition that modifies our conduct towards the external world; and if we find this antagonistic, it is because we are at war with ourselves, w_th the essential laws of our mind and our heart. The attitude of Nature towards us is uninfluenced by the justice or injustice of our intentions; and yet these will almost invariably govern our attitude towards Nature. Here once more, as in the case of social justice, we ascribe to the universe, to an unintelligible, eternal, fatal principle, a part that we play ourselves; and when we say that justice, heaven, nature, or events are rising in revolt against us to punish or to avenge, it is in reality man who is using events to punish man, it is human nature that rises in revolt, and human justice that avenges.

16

In a former essay I referred to Napoleon's three crowning acts of injustice: the three celebrated crimes that were so fatally unjust to his own fortune. The first was the murder of the Duc d'Enghien, condemned by order, without trial or proof, and executed in the trenches of Vincennes; an assassination that sowed insatiable hatred and vengeance in the path of the guilty dictator. Then the detestable intrigues whereby he lured the too trustful, easy-going Bourbons to Bayonne, that he might rob them of their hereditary crown; and the horrible war that ensued, a war that cost the lives of three hundred thousand men, swallowed up all the morality and energy of the empire, most of its prestige, almost all its convictions, almost all the devotion it inspired, and engulfed its prosperous destiny. And finally the frightful, unpardonable Russian campaign, wherein his fortune came at last to utter shipwreck amid the ice of the Berezina and the snow-bound Polish steppes.

"These prodigious catastrophes," I said, "had numberless causes; but when we have slowly traced our way through all the more or less unforeseen circumstances, and have marked the gradual change in Napoleon's character, have noted the acts of imprudence, folly, and violence which this genius committed; when we have seen how deliberately he brought disaster to his smiling fortune, may we not almost believe that what we behold, standing erect at the very fountain-head of calamity, is no other than the silent shadow of misunderstood human justice? Human justice, wherein there is nothing supernatural, nothing very mysterious, but built up of many thousand very real little incidents, many thousand falsehoods, many thousand little offences of which each one gave rise to a corresponding act of retaliation—human justice, and not a power that suddenly, at some tragic moment, leaps forth like Minerva of old, fully armed, from the formidable, despotic brow of destiny. In all this there is only one thing of mystery, and that is the eternal presence of human justice; but we are aware that the nature of man is very mysterious. Let us in the meanwhile ponder this mystery. It is the most certain of all, it is the profoundest, it is the most helpful, it is the only one that will never paralyse our energy for good And though that patient, vigilant shadow be not as clearly defined in every life as it was in Napoleon's, though justice be not always as active or as undeniable, we shall none the less do wisely to study a case like this whenever opportunity offers. It will at least give rise to doubt within us, it will stimulate inquiry; and these things are worth far more than the idle, short-sighted affirmation or denial that we so often permit ourselves: for in all questions of this kind our endeavour should not be to prove, but rather to arouse attention, to create a certain grave, courageous respect for all that yet remains unexplained in the actions of men, in their subjection to what appear to be general laws, and in the results that ensue."

17

Let us now try to discover in what way this great mystery of justice does truly and inevitably work itself out within us. The heart of him who has committed an unjust act becomes the scene of ineffaceable drama, the paramount drama of human nature; and it becomes the more dangerous, and deadlier, in the degree of the man's greatness and knowledge.

A Napoleon will say to himself, at such troubled moments, that the morality of a great life cannot be as simple as that of an ordinary one, and that an active, powerful will has rights which the feeble, inert will cannot claim. He will hold that he may the more legitimately sweep aside certain conscientious scruples, inasmuch as it is not ignorance or weakness that causes him to disregard these, but the fact that he views them from a standpoint higher than that of the majority of men; and further, that his aim being great and glorious, this passing deliberate callousness of his is therefore truly a victory won by his strength and his intellect, since there can be no danger in doing wrong when it is done by one who does it knowingly, and has his very good reason. All this, however, does not for a moment delude that which lies deepest within us. An act of injustice must always shake the confidence a man had in himself and his destiny; at a given moment, and that generally of the gravest, he has ceased to rely upon himself alone; and this will not be forgotten, nor will he ever again be wholly himself. He has confused, and probably corrupted, his fortune by the introduction of strange powers. He has lost the exact sense of his personality and of the force that is in him. He can no longer clearly distinguish between what is his own and comes from himself, and what he is constantly borrowing from the pernicious collaborators whom his weakness has summoned. He has ceased to be the general who has none but disciplined soldiers in the army of his thoughts; he becomes the usurping chief around whom are only accomplices. He has forsworn the dignity of the man who will have none of the glory at which his heart can only smile as sadly as an ardent, unhappy lover will smile at a faithless mistress.

He who is truly strong will examine with eager care the praise and advantages that his actions have won for him, and will silently reject whatever oversteps a certain line that he has drawn in his consciousness. And the stronger he is, the more nearly will this line approach the one that has already been drawn by the secret truth that lies at the bottom of all things. An act of injustice is almost always a confession of weakness; and very few such confessions are needed to reveal to the enemy the most vulnerable spot of the soul. He who commits an unjust deed that he may gain some measure of glory, or preserve the little glory he has, does but admit that what he desires or what he possesses is beyond his deserving, and that the part he has sought to play exceeds his powers of loyal fulfilment. And if, notwithstanding all, he persist in his endeavour, his life will soon be beset by falsehoods, errors, and phantoms.

And at last, after a few acts of weakness, of treachery, of culpable self-indulgence, the survey of our past life can bring discouragement only, whereas we have great need that our past should inspire and sustain us. For therein alone do we truly know what we are; it is only our past that can come to us, in our moments of doubt, and say: "Since you were able to do that thing, it shall lie in your power to do this thing also. When that danger confronted you, when that terrible grief laid you prostrate, you had faith in yourself, and you conquered. The conditions to-day are the same; do you but preserve your faith in yourself, and your star will be constant." But what reply shall we make if our past can only whisper: "Your success has been solely due to injustice and falsehood, wherefore it behoves you once more to deceive and to lie"? No man cares to let his eyes rest on his acts of disloyalty, weakness, or treachery; and all the events of bygone days which we cannot contemplate calmly and peacefully, with satisfaction and confidence, trouble and restrict the horizon which the days that are not yet are forming far away. It is only a prolonged survey of the past that can give to the eye the strength it needs in order to sound the future.

18

No, it was not the inherent justice of things that punished Napoleon for his three great acts of injustice, or that will punish us for our own in a less startling, but not less painful, fashion. Nor was it an unyielding, incorruptible, irresistible justice, "attaining the very vault of heaven." We are punished because our entire moral being, our mind no less than our character, is incapable of living and acting except in justice. Leaving that, we leave our natural element; we are carried, as it were, into a planet of which we know nothing, where the ground slips from under our feet, and all things disconcert us; for while the humblest intellect feels itself at home in justice, and can readily foretell the consequences of every just act, the most profound and penetrating mind loses its way hopelessly in the injustice itself has created, and can form no conception of what results shall ensue. The man of genius who forsakes the equity that the humble peasant has at heart will find all paths strange to him; and these will be stranger still should he overstep the limit his own sense of justice imposes: for the justice that soars aloft, keeping pace with the intellect, creates new boundaries around all it throws open, while at the same time strengthening and rendering more insurmountable still the ancient barriers of instinct. The moment we cross the primitive frontier of equity all things seem to fail us; one falsehood gives birth to a hundred, and treachery returns to us through a thousand channels. If justice be in us we may march along boldly, for there are certain things to which the basest cannot be false; but if injustice possess us we must beware of the justest of men, for there are things to which even these cannot remain faithful. As our physical organism was devised for existence in the atmosphere of our globe, so is our moral organism devised for existence in justice. Every faculty craves for it, and is more intimately bound up with it than with the laws of gravitation, of light or heat; and to throw ourselves into injustice is to plunge headlong into the hostile and the unknown. All that is in us has been placed there with a view to justice; all things tend thither and urge us towards it: whereas, when we harbour injustice, we battle against our own strength; and at last, at the hour of inevitable punishment, when, prostrate, weeping and penitent, we recognise that events, the sky, the universe, the invisible are all in rebellion, all justly in league against us, then may we truly say, not that these are, or ever have been, just, but that we, notwithstanding ourselves, have contrived to remain just even in our injustice.

19

We affirm that Nature is absolutely indifferent to our morality, and that were this morality to command us to kill our neighbour, or to do him the utmost possible harm, Nature would aid us in this no less than in our endeavour to comfort or serve him. She as often would seem to reward us for having made him suffer as for our kindness towards him.

Maurice Maeterlinck

Does this warrant the inference that Nature has no morality —using the word in its most limited sense as meaning the logical, inevitable subordination of the means to the accomplishment of a general mission? This is a question to which we must not too hastily reply. We know nothing of Nature's aim, or even whether she have an aim. We know nothing of her consciousness, or whether she have a consciousness; of her thoughts, or whether she think at all. It is with her deeds and her manner of doing that we are solely concerned. And in these we find the same contradiction between our morality and Nature's mode of action as exists between our consciousness and the instincts that Nature has planted within us. For this consciousness, though in ultimate analysis due to her also, has nevertheless been formed by ourselves, and, basing itself upon the loftiest human morality, offers an ever stronger opposition to the desires of instinct. Were we to listen only to these last, we should act in all things like Nature, which would invariably seem to justify the triumph of the stronger, the victory of the least scrupulous and best equipped; and this in the midst of the most inexcusable wars, the most flagrant acts of injustice or cruelty. Our one object would be our own personal triumph; nor should we pay the least heed to the rights or sufferings of our victims, to their innocence or beauty, moral or intellectual superiority. But, in that case, why has Nature placed within us a consciousness and a sense of justice that have prevented us from desiring those things that she desires? Or is it we ourselves who have placed them there? Are we capable of deriving from within us something that is not in Nature; are we capable of giving abnormal development to a force that opposes her force; and if we possess this power, must not Nature have reasons of her own for permitting us to possess it? Why should there be only in us, and nowhere else in the world, these two irreconcilable tendencies, that in every man are incessantly at strife, and alternately victorious? Would one have been dangerous without the other? Would it have overstepped its goal, perhaps; would the desire for conquest, unchecked by the sense of justice, have led to annihilation, as the sense of justice without the desire for conquest might have lured us to inertia? Which of these two tendencies is the more natural and necessary, which is the narrower and which the vaster, which is provisional and which eternal? Where shall we learn which one we should combat and which one encourage? Ought we to conform to the law that is incontestably the more general, or should we cherish in our heart a law that is evidently exceptional? Are there circumstances under which we have the right to go forth in search of the apparent ideal of life? Is it our duty to follow the morality of the species or race, which seems irresistible to us, being one of the visible sides of Nature's obscure and unknown intentions; or is it essential that the individual should maintain and develop within him a morality entirely opposed to that of the race or species whereof he forms part?

20

The truth is that the question which confronts us here is only another form of the one which lies at the root of evolutionary morality, and is probably scientifically unsolvable. Evolutionary morality bases itself on the justice of Nature—though it dare not speak out the word; on the justice of Nature, which imposes upon each individual the good or evil consequences of his own character and his own actions. But when, on the other hand, it is necessary for evolutionary morality to justify actions which, although intrinsically unjust, are necessary for the prosperity of the species, it falls back upon what it reluctantly terms Nature's indifference or injustice. Here we have two unknown aims, that of humanity and that of Nature; and these, wrapped as they are in a mystery that may some day perhaps pass away, would seem to be irreconcilable in our mind. Essentially, all these questions resolve themselves into one, which is of the utmost importance to our contemporary morality. The race would appear to be becoming conscious, prematurely it may be, and perhaps disastrously, not, we will say, of its rights, for that problem is still in suspense, but of the fact that morality does not enter into certain actions that go to make history.

This disquieting consciousness would seem to be slowly invading our individual life. Thrice, and more or less in the course of one year, has this question confronted us, and assumed vast proportions: in the matter of America's crushing defeat of Spain (although here the issues were confused, for the Spaniards, besides their present blunders, had been guilty of so many acts of injustice in the past, that the problem becomes very involved); in the case of an innocent man sacrificed to the preponderating interests of his country; and in the iniquitous war of the Transvaal. It is true that the phenomenon is not altogether without precedent. Man has always endeavoured to justify his injustice; and when human justice offered him no excuse or pretext, he found in the will of the gods a law superior to the justice of man. But our excuse or pretext of to-day is fraught with the more peril to our morality inasmuch as it reposes on a law, or at least a habit, of Nature, that is far more real, more incontestable and universal than the will of an ephemeral and local god.

Which shall prevail in the end, justice or force? Does force contain an unknown justice that will absorb our human justice, or is the impulse of justice within us, that would seem to resist blind force, actually no more than a devious emanation from that force, tending to the same end; and is it only the point of deviation that escapes us? This is not a question that we can answer, we who ourselves form part of the mystery we seek to solve; the reply could come only from one who might be gazing upon us from the heights of another world: one who should have learned the aim of the universe and the destiny of man. In the meanwhile, if we say that Nature is right, we say that the instinct of justice, which she has placed in us, and which therefore also is nature, is wrong; whereas if we approve this instinct, our approval is necessarily derived from the exercise of the very faculty that is called in question.

21

That is true; but it is no less true that the endeavour to sum up the world in a syllogism is one of the oldest and vainest habits of man. In the region of the unknown and unknow-able, logic-chopping has its perils; and in the present case all our doubts would seem to arise from another hazardous syllogism. We tell ourselves—boldly at times, but more often in a whisper—that we are Nature's children, and bound therefore in all things to conform to her laws and copy her example. And since Nature regards justice with indifference, since she has another aim, which is the sustaining, the renewing, the incessant development of life, it follows. . . . So far we have not formulated the conclusion, or, at least, this conclusion has not yet openly dared to force its way into our morality; but, although its influence has hitherto only been remotely felt in that familiar sphere which includes our relations, our friends, and our immediate surroundings, it is slowly penetrating into the vast and desolate region whither we relegate all those whom we know not and see not, who for us have no name. It is already to be found at the root of many of our actions; it has entered our politics, our industry, our commerce; indeed it affects almost all we do from the moment we emerge from the narrow circle of our domestic hearth, the only place for the majority of men where a little veritable justice is still to be found, a little benevolence, a little love. It will call itself economic or social law, evolution, competition, struggle for life; it will masquerade under a thousand names, forever perpetrating the selfsame wrong. And yet nothing can be less legitimate than such a conclusion. Apart from the fact that we might with equal justification reverse the syllogism, and cause it to declare that there must be a certain justice in Nature, since we, her children, are just, we need only consider it as it stands to realise how doubtful and contestable is at least one of its premisses.

We have seen in the preceding chapters that Nature does not appear to be just from our point of view; but we have absolutely no means of judging whether she be not just from her own. The fact that she pays no heed to the morality of our actions does not warrant the inference that she has no morality, or that ours is the only one there can be. We are entitled to say that she is indifferent as to whether our intentions be good or evil, but have not the right to conclude that she has therefore no morality and no equity; for that would be tantamount to affirming that there are no more mysteries or secrets, and that we know all the laws of the universe, its origin and its end. Her mode of action is different from our own, but, I say it once more, we know not what her reason may be for acting in this different fashion; and we have no right to imitate what seems to us iniquitous and cruel, so long as we have no precise knowledge of the profound and salutary reasons that may underlie such action. What is the aim of Nature? Whither do the worlds tend that stretch across eternity? Where does consciousness begin, and is its only form that which it assumes in ourselves? At what point do physical laws become moral laws? Is life unintelligent? Have we sounded all the depths of Nature, and is it only in our cerebro-spinal system that she becomes mind? And finally, what is justice when viewed from other heights? Is the intention necessarily at its centre; and can no regions exist where intentions no longer shall count? We should have to answer these questions, and many others, before we could tell whether Nature be just or unjust from the point of view of masses whose vastness corresponds to her own. She disposes of a future, a space, of which we can form no conception; and in these there exists, it may be, a justice proportioned to her duration, to her extent and aim, even as our own instinct of justice is proportioned to the duration and narrow circle of our own life. The wrong that she may for centuries commit she has centuries wherein to repair; but we, who have only a few days before us, what right have we to imitate what our eye cannot see, understand, or follow? By what standard are we to judge her, if we look away from the passing hour? For instance, considering only the imperceptible speck that we form in the worlds, and disregarding the immensity that surrounds us, we are wholly ignorant of all that concerns our possible life beyond the tomb; and we forget that, in the present state of our knowledge, nothing authorises us to affirm that there may not be a kind of more or less conscious, more or less responsible after-life, that shall in no way depend on the decisions of an external will. He would indeed be rash who should venture to maintain that nothing survives, either in us or in others, of the efforts of our good intentions and the acquirements of our mind. It may be—and serious experiments, though they do not seem to prove the phenomenon, may still allow us to class it among scientific possibilities—it may be that a part of our personality, of our nervous force, may escape dissolution. How vast a future would then be thrown open to the laws that unite cause to effect, and that always end by creating justice when they come into contact with the human soul, and have centuries before them! Let us not forget that Nature at least is logical, even though we call her unjust; and were we to resolve on injustice, our difficulty would be that we must also be logical; and when logic comes into touch with our thoughts and our feelings, our intentions and passions, what is there that differentiates it from justice?

22

Let us form no too hasty conclusion; too many points are still uncertain. Should we seek to imitate what we term the injustice of Nature, we would run the risk of imitating and fostering only the injustice that is in ourselves. When we say that Nature is unjust, we are in effect complaining of her indifference to our own little virtues, our own little intentions, our own little deeds of heroism; and it is our vanity, far more than our sense of equity, that considers itself aggrieved. Our morality is proportioned to our stature and our restricted destiny; nor have we the right to forsake it because it is not on the scale of the immensity and infinite destiny of the universe.

And further, should it even be proved that Nature is unjust at all points, the other question remains intact: whether the command be laid upon man to follow Nature in her injustice. Here we shall do well to let our own consciousness speak, rather than listen to a voice so formidable that we hear not a word it utters, and are not even certain whether words there be. Reason and instinct tell us that it is right to follow the counsels of Nature; but they tell us also that we should not follow those counsels when they clash with another instinct within us, one that is no less profound: the instinct of the just and the unjust. And if instincts do indeed draw very near to the truth of Nature, and must be respected by us in the degree of the force that is in them, this one is perhaps the strongest of all, for it has struggled alone against all the others combined, and still persists within us. Nor is this the hour to reject it. Until other certitudes reach us, it behoves us, who are men, to continue just in the human way and the human sphere. We do not see far enough, or clearly enough, to be just in another sphere. Let us not venture into a kind of abyss, out of which races and peoples to come may perhaps find a passage, but whereinto man, in so far as he is man, must not seek to penetrate. The injustice of Nature ends by becoming justice for the race; she has time before her, she can wait, her injustice is of her girth. But for us it is too overwhelming, and our days are too few. Let us be satisfied that force should reign in the universe, but equity in our heart. Though the race be irresistibly, and perhaps justly, unjust, though even the crowd appear possessed of rights denied to the isolated man, and commit on occasions great, inevitable, and salutary crimes, it is still the duty of each individual of the race, of every member of the crowd, to remain just, while ever adding to and sustaining the consciousness within him. Nor shall we be entitled to abandon this duty till all the reasons of the great apparent injustice be known to us; and those that are given us now, preservation of the species, reproduction and selection of the strongest, ablest, "fittest," are not sufficient to warrant so frightful a change. Let each one try by all means to become the strongest, most skilful, the best adapted to the necessities of the life that he cannot transform; but, so far, the qualities that shall enable him to conquer, that shall give the fullest play to his moral power and his intelligence, and shall truly make him the happiest, most skilful, the strongest, and "fittest"—these qualities are precisely the ones that are the most human, the most honourable, and the most just.

23

"Within me there is more," runs the fine device inscribed on the beams and pediment of an old patrician mansion at Bruges, which every traveller visits; filling a corner of one of those tender and melancholy quays, that are as forlorn and lifeless as though they existed only on canvas. And so too might man exclaim, "Within me there is more;" every law of morality, every intelligible mystery. There may be many others, above us and below us; but if these are to remain for ever unknown, they become for us as though they were not; and should their existence one day be revealed to us; it can only be because they already are in us, already are ours. "Within me there is more;" and we are entitled to add, perhaps, "I have nothing to fear from that which is in me."

This much at least is certain, that the one active, inhabited region of the mystery of justice is to be found within ourselves. Other regions lack consistency; they are probably imaginary, and must inevitably be deserted and sterile. They may have furnished mankind with illusions that served some purpose, but not always without doing harm; and though we may scarcely be entitled to demand that all illusions should be destroyed, they should at least not be too manifestly opposed to our conception of the universe. To-day we seek in all things the illusion of truth. It is not the last, perhaps, or the best, or the only one possible; but it is the one which we at present regard as the most honourable and the most necessary. Let us limit ourselves therefore to recognising the admirable love of justice and truth that exists in the heart of man. Proceeding thus, yielding admiration only where it is incontestably due, we shall gradually acquire some knowledge of this passion, which is the distinguishing note of man; and one thing, most important of all, we shall most undoubtedly learn—the means whereby we can purify it, and still further increase it. As we observe its incessant activity in the depths of our heart, the only temple where it can truly be active: as we watch it blending with all that we think, and feel, and do, we shall quickly discover which are the things that throw light upon it, and which those that plunge it in darkness; which are the things that guide it, and which those that lead it astray; we shall learn what nourishes it and what atrophies, what defends and what attacks.

Is justice no more than the human instinct of preservation and defence? Is it the purest product of our reason; or rather to be regarded as composed of a number of those sentimental forces which so often are right, though directly opposed to our reason—forces that in themselves are a kind of unconscious, vaster reason, to which our conscious reason invariably accords its startled approval when it has reached the heights whence those kindly feelings long had beheld what itself was unable to see? Is justice dependent on intellect, or rather on character? Questions, these, that are perhaps not idle if we indeed would know what steps we must take to invest with all its radiance and all its power the love of justice that is the central jewel of the human soul. All men love justice, but not with the same ardent, fierce, and exclusive love; nor have they all the same scruples, the same sensitiveness, or the same deep conviction. We meet people of highly developed intellect in whom the sense of what is just and unjust is yet infinitely less delicate, less clearly marked, than in others whose intellect would seem to be mediocre; for here a great part is played by that little-known, ill-defined side of ourselves that we term the character. And yet it is difficult to tell how much more or less unconscious intellect must of necessity go with the character that is unaffectedly honest. The point before us, however, is to learn how best to illumine, and increase within us, our desire for justice; and it is certain that, at the start, our character is less directly influenced by the desire for justice than is our intellect, the development of which this desire in a large measure controls; and the co-operation of the intellect, which recognises and encourages our good intention, is necessary for this intention to penetrate into, and mould, our character. That portion of our love of justice, therefore, which depends on our character, will benefit by its passage through the intellect; for in proportion as the intellect rises, and acquires enlightenment, will it succeed in mastering, enlightening, and transforming our instincts and our feelings.

But let us no longer believe that this love must be sought in a kind of superhuman, and often inhuman, infinite. None of the grandeur and beauty that this infinite may possess would fall to its portion; it would only be incoherent, inactive, and vague. Whereas by seeking it in ourselves, where it truly is; by observing it there, listening to it, marking how it profits by every acquirement of our mind, every joy and sorrow of our heart, we soon shall learn what we best had do to purify and increase it.

24

Our task within these limits will be sufficiently long and mysterious. To increase and purify within us the desire for justice: how shall this thing be done? We have some vague conception of the ideal that we would approach; but how changeable still, and illusory, is this ideal! It is lessened by all that is still unknown to us in the universe, by all that we do not perceive or perceive incompletely, by all that we question too superficially. It is hedged round by the most insidious dangers; it falls victim to the strangest oblivion, the most inconceivable blunders. Of all our ideals it is the one that we should watch with the greatest care and anxiety, with the most passionate, pious eagerness and solicitude. What seems irreproachably just to us at the moment is probably the merest fraction of what would seem just could we shift our point of view. We need only compare what we were doing yesterday with what we do to-day; and what we do to-day would appear full of faults against equity, were it granted to us to rise still higher, and compare it with what we shall do to-morrow. There needs but a passing event, a thought that uses, a duty to ourselves that takes definite form, an unexpected responsibility that is suddenly made clear, for the whole organisation of our inward justice to totter and be transformed. Slow as our advance may have been, we still should find it impossible to begin life over again in the midst of many a sorrow whereof we were the involuntary cause, many a discouragement to which we unconsciously gave rise; and yet, when these things came into being around us, we appeared to be in the right, and did not consider ourselves unjust. And even so are we convinced to-day of our excellent intentions, even so do we tell ourselves that we are the cause if no suffering and no tears, that we stay not a murmur of happiness, shorten no moment of peace or of love; and it may be that there passes, unperceived of us, to our right or our left, an illimitable injustice that spreads over three-fourths of our life.

25

I chanced to-day to take up a copy of the "Arabian Nights," in the very remarkable translation recently published by Dr. Mardrus; and I marvelled at the extraordinary picture it gives of the ancient, long-vanished civilisations. Not in the Odyssey or the Bible, in Xenophon or Plutarch, could their teaching be more clearly set forth. There is one story that the Sultana Schahrazade tells—it is one of the very finest the volume contains—that reveals a life as pure and as admirable as mankind ever has known; a life replete with beauty, happiness, and love; spontaneous and vivid, intelligent, nourishing, and refined; an abundant life that, to a certain point, comes as near truth as a life well can. It is, in many respects, almost as perfect in its moral as in its material civilisation. And the pillars on which this incomparable structure of happiness rests—like pillars of light supporting the light—are formed of ideas of justice so exquisitely delicate, counsels of wisdom so deeply penetrating, that we of to-day, being less fine in grain, less eager and buoyant, have lost the power to formulate, or to discern, them. And for all that, this abode of felicity, that harbours a moral life so active and vigorous, so graciously grave, so noble—this palace, wherein the purest and holiest wisdom governs the pleasures of rejoicing mankind, is in its entirety based on so great an injustice, is enclosed by so vast, so profound, so frightful an iniquity, that the wretchedest man of us all would shrink in dismay from its glittering, gem-bestrewn threshold. But of this iniquity they who linger in that marvellous dwelling have not the remotest suspicion. It would seem that they never draw near to a window; or that, should one by some chance fly open and reveal to their sorrowful gaze the misery strewn in the midst of the revels and feasting, they still would be blind to the crime which was infinitely more revolting, infinitely more monstrous, than the most appalling poverty—the crime of the slavery, and the even more terrible degradation, of their women. For these, however exalted their position, and at the moment even when they are speaking to the men round about them of goodness and justice—when they are reminding them of their most touching and generous duties—these women never are more than objects of pleasure, to be bought or sold, or given away in a moment of gratitude, ostentation, or drunkenness, to any barbarous or hideous master.

26

"They tell us," says the beautiful slave Nozhatan, as, concealed behind a curtain of silk and of pearls, she speaks to Prince Sharkan and the wise men of the kingdom; "they tell us that the Khalif Omar set forth one night, in the company of the venerable Aslam Abou-Zeid, and that he beheld, far away from his palace, a fire that was burning; and drew near, as he thought that his presence might perhaps be of service. And he saw a poor woman who was kindling wood underneath a cauldron; and by her side were two little wretched children, groaning most piteously. And Omar said,

'Peace unto thee, O woman! What dost thou here, alone in the night and the cold?' And she answered, 'Lord, I am making this water to boil, that my children may drink, who perish of hunger and cold; but for the misery we have to bear Allah will surely one day ask reckoning of Omar the Khalif.' And the Khalif, who was in disguise, was much moved, and he said to her, 'But dost thou think, O woman, that Omar can know of thy wretchedness, since he does not relieve it?' And she answered, 'Wherefore then is Omar the Khalif, if he be unaware of the misery of his people and of each one of his subjects?' Then the Khalif was silent, and he said to Aslam Abou-Zeid, 'Let us go quickly from hence.' And he hastened until he had reached the storehouse of his kitchens, and he entered therein and drew forth a sack of flour from the midst of the other sacks, and also a jar that was filled to the brim with sheep-fat, and he said to Abou-Zeid, 'O Abou-Zeid, help thou me to charge these on my back.' But Abou-Zeid refused, and he cried, 'Suffer that I carry them on my back, O Commander of the Faithful.' And Omar said calmly to him, 'Wilt thou also, O Abou-Zeid, bear the weight of my sins on the day of resurrection?' And Abou-Zeid was obliged to lay the jar filled with fat, and the sack of flour, on the Khalif's back. And Omar hastened, thus laden, until he had once again reached the poor woman; and he took of the flour, and he took of the fat, and placed these in the cauldron, over the fire; and with his own hands did he then get ready the food, and he quickened the fire with his breath; and as he bent over, his beard being long, the smoke from the wood forced its way through the beard of the Khalif. And at last, when the food was prepared, Omar offered it unto the woman and the two little children; and with his breath did he cool the food while they ate their fill. Then he left them the sack of flour and the jar of fat; and he went on his way, and said unto Aslam Abou-Zeid, 'O Abou-Zeid, the light from this fire I have seen to-day has enlightened me also.'"

27

And it is thus that, a little further on, there speaks to a very wise king one of five pensive maidens whom this king is invited to purchase: "Know thou, O king," she says, "that the most beautiful deed one can do is the deed that is disinterested. And so do they tell us that in Israel once were two brothers. and that one asked the other, 'Of all the deeds thou hast done, which was the most wicked?' And his brother replied, 'This. As I passed a hen-roost one day, I stretched out my arm and I seized a chicken and strangled it, and then flung it back into the roost. That is the wickedest deed of my life. And thou, O my brother, what is thy wickedest action?' And he answered, 'That I prayed to Allah one day to demand a favour of him. For it is only when the soul is simply uplifted on high that prayer can be beautiful.'"

And one of her companions, captive and slave like herself, also speaks to the king: "Learn to know thyself," she says. "Learn to know thyself! And do thou not act till then. And do thou then only act in accordance with all thy desires, but having great care always that thou do not injure thy neighbour."

To this last formula our morality of today has nothing to add; nor can we conceive a precept that shall be more complete. At most we could widen somewhat the meaning of the word "neighbour," and raise, render somewhat more subtle and more elastic. that of the word "injure." And the book in which these words are found is a monument of horror, not-withstanding all its flowers and all its wisdom a monument of horror and blood and tears, of despotism and slavery. And they who pronounce these words are slaves. A merchant buys them I know not where, and sells them to some old hag who teaches them, or causes them to be taught, philosophy, poetry, all Eastern sciences, in order that one day they may become gifts worthy of a king. And when their education is finished, and their beauty and wisdom call forth the admiration of all who approach them, the industrious, prudent old woman does indeed offer them to a very wise, very just king. And when this very wise, very just king has taken their virginity from them, and seeks other loves, he will probably bestow them (I have forgotten the end of this particular story, but it is the invariable destiny of all the heroines of these marvellous legends) on his viziers. And these viziers will give them away in exchange for a vase of perfume or a belt studded with jewels; or perhaps despatch them to a distant country, there to conciliate a powerful protector, or a hideous, but dreaded, rival. And these women, so fully conscious of themselves, whose gaze can penetrate so deeply into the consciousness of others—these women who forever are pondering the loftiest, grandest problems of justice, of the morality of men and of nations—never throw one questioning glance on their fate, or for an instant suspect the abominable injustice whereof they are the victims. Nor do those suspect it either who listen to them, and love and admire them, and understand them. And we who marvel at this—we who also reflect on justice and virtue, on pity and love—are we so sure that they who come after us shall not some day find, in our present social condition, a spectacle no less disconcerting?

28

It is difficult for us to imagine what the ideal justice will be, for every thought of ours that tends towards it is clogged by the injustice wherein we still live. Who shall say what new laws or relations will stand revealed when the misfortunes and inequalities due to the action of man shall have been swept away; when, in accordance with the principles of evolutionary morality, each individual shall "reap the results, good or bad, of his own nature, and of the consequences that ensue from that nature"? At present things happen otherwise; and we may unhesitatingly declare that, as far as the material condition of the vast bulk of mankind is concerned, the connection between conduct and consequences—to use Spencer's formula—exists only in the most ludicrous, arbitrary, and iniquitous fashion. Is there not some audacity in our imagining that our thoughts can possibly be just when the body of each one of us is steeped to the neck in injustice? And from this injustice no man is free, be it to his loss or his gain: there is not one whose efforts are not disproportion-ately rewarded, receiving too much or too little; not one who is not either advantaged or handicapped. And endeavour as we may to detach our mind from this inveterate injustice, this lingering trace of the sub-human morality needful for primitive races, it is idle to think that our thoughts can be as strenuous, independent, or clear as they might have been had the last vestige of this injustice disappeared; it is idle to think that they can achieve the same result. The side of the human mind that can attain a region loftier than reality is necessarily timid and hesitating. Human thought is capable of many things; it has, in the course of time, brought startling improvement to bear upon what seemed immutable in the species or the race. But even at the moment when it is pondering the transformation of which it has caught a distant glimpse, the improvement that it so eagerly desires, even then it is still thinking, feeling, seeing like the thing that it seeks to alter, even then it lies captive beneath the yoke. All its efforts notwithstanding, it is practically that which it would change. For the mind of man lacks the power to forecast the future; it has been formed rather to explain, judge, and co-ordinate that which was, to help, foster, and make known what already exists, but so far cannot be seen; and when it ventures into what is not yet, it will rarely produce anything very salutary or very enduring. And the influence of the social condition in which we exist lies heavy upon it. How can we frame a satisfactory idea of justice, and ponder it loyally, with the needful tranquillity, when injustice surrounds us on every side? Before we can study justice, or speak of it with advantage, it must become what it is capable of being: a social force, irreproachable and actual. At present all we can do is to invoke its unconscious, secret, and, as it were, almost imperceptible efforts. We contemplate it from the shores of human injustice; never yet has it been granted us to gaze on the open sea beneath the illimitable, inviolate sky of a conscience without reproach. If men had at least done all that it was possible for them to do in their own domain, they would then have the right to go further, and question elsewhere; and their thoughts would probably be clearer, were their consciences more at ease.

29

And further, a heavy reproach lies on us and chills our ardour whenever we try to grow better, to increase our knowledge, our love, our forgiveness. Though we purify our consciousness and ennoble our thoughts, though we strive to render life softer and sweeter for those who are near us, all our efforts halt at our threshold, and have no influence on what lies outside our door; and the moment we leave our home we feel that we have done nothing, that there is nothing for us to do, and that we are taking part, ourselves notwithstanding, in the great anonymous injustice. Is it not almost ludicrous that we, who within our four walls strive to be noble and faithful, pitiful, simple and loyal; we whose consciousness balances the nicest, most delicate problems, and rejects even the suspicion of a bitter thought, have no sooner gone into the street and met faces that are unfamiliar, than, at that very instant, and without the least possibility of our having it otherwise, all pity, equity, love, should be completely ignored by us? What dignity, what loyalty, can there be in this double life, so wise and humane, uplifted and thoughtful, this side the threshold, and beyond it so callous, so instinctive and pitiless! For it is enough that we should feel the cold a little less than the labourer who passes by, that we should be better fed or clad than he, that we should buy any object that is not strictly indispensable, and we have unconsciously returned, through a thousand byways, to the ruthless act of primitive man despoiling his weaker brother. There is no single privilege we enjoy but close investigation will prove it to be the result of a perhaps very remote abuse of power, of an unknown violence or ruse of long ago; and all these we set in motion again as we sit at our table, stroll idly through the town, or lie at night in a bed that our own hands have not made. Nay, what is even the leisure that enables us to improve, to grow more compassionate and gentler, to think more fraternally of the injustice others endure—what is this, in truth, but the ripest fruit of the great injustice?

30

These scruples, I know, must not be carried too far: they would either induce a spirit of useless revolt, possibly disastrous to the species whose mild and mighty sluggishness we are bound to respect; or they would lead us back to I know not what mystic, inert renouncement, directly opposed to the most evident and unchanging desires of life. Life has laws that we call inevitable; but we are already becoming more sparing in our use of the word. And here especially do we note the change that has come over the attitude of the wise and upright man. Marcus Aurelius—than whom perhaps none ever craved more earnestly for justice, or possessed a soul more wisely impressionable, more nobly sensitive—Marcus Aurelius never asked himself what might be happening outside that admirable little circle of light wherein his virtue and consciousness, his divine meekness and piety, had gathered those who were near him, his friends and his servants. Infinite iniquity, he knew full well, stretched around him on every side; but with this he had no concern. To him it seemed a thing that must be, a thing mysterious and sacred as the mighty ocean; the boundless domain of the gods, of fatality, of laws unknown and superior, irresistible, irresponsible, and eternal. It did not lessen his courage; on the contrary, it enhanced his confidence, his concentration, and spurred him upwards, like the flame that, confined to a narrow area, rises higher and higher, alone in the night, urged on by the darkness. He accepted the decree of fate, that allotted slavery to the bulk of mankind. Sorrowfully but with full conviction, did he submit to the irrevocable law; wherein he once again gave proof of his piety and his virtue. He retired into himself, and there, in a kind of sunless, motionless void, became still more just, still more humane. And in each succeeding century do we find a similar ardour, self-centred and solitary, among those who were wise and good. The name of more than one immovable law might change, but its infinite part remained ever the same; and each one regarded it with the like resigned and chastened melancholy. But we of to-day— what course are we to pursue? We know that iniquity is no longer necessary. We have invaded the region of the gods, of destiny, and unknown laws. These may still control disease or accident, perhaps, no less than the tempest, the lightning-flash, and most of the mysteries of death—we have not yet penetrated to them—but we are well aware that poverty, wretchedness, hopeless toil, slavery, famine, are completely outside their domain. It is we who organise these, we who maintain and distribute them. These frightful scourges, that have grown so familiar, are wielded by us alone; and belief in their superhuman origin is becoming rarer and rarer. The religious, impassable ocean, that excused and protected the retreat into himself of the sage and the man of good, now

Maurice Maeterlinck

only exists as a vague recollection. To-day Marcus Aurelius could no longer say with the same serenity: "They go in search of refuges, of rural cottages, of mountains and the seashore; thou too art wont to cherish an eager desire for these things. But is this not the act of an ignorant, unskilled man, seeing that it is granted thee at whatever hour thou pleasest to retire within thyself? It is not possible for man to discover a retreat more tranquil, less disturbed by affairs, than that which he finds in his soul; especially if he have within him those things the contemplation of which suffices to procure immediate enjoyment of the perfect calm, which is no other, to my mind, than the perfect agreement of soul."

Other matters concern us to-day than this agreement of soul; or let us rather say that what we have to do is to bring into agreement there that from which the soul of Marcus Aurelius was free—three-fourths of the sorrows of mankind, in a word—which have become real to us, intelligible, human, and urgent, and are no longer regarded as the inexplicable, immutable, intangible decrees of fatality.

31

This does not imply, however, that we should abandon the old sages' desire for "agreement"; and even though we may not be entitled to expect such perfect "agreement" as they derived from their pardonable egoism, we may still look for agreement of a provisional, conditional kind. And although such "agreement" be not the last word of morality, it is none the less indispensable that we should begin by being as just as we possibly can within ourselves and to those round about us, our neighbours, our friends, and our servants. It is at the moment when we have become absolutely just to these, and within our own consciousness, that we realise our great injustice to all the others. The method of being more practically just towards these last is not yet known to us; to return to great, heroic renouncements would effect but little, for these are incapable of unanimous action, and would probably run counter to the profoundest laws of nature, which rejects renouncement in every form save that of maternal love.

This practical justice, therefore, remains the secret of the race. Of such secrets it has many, which it reveals one by one, at such moments of history as become truly critical; and the solutions it offers to insuperable difficulties are almost always unexpected, and of strangest simplicity. The hour approaches, perhaps, when it will speak once more. Let us hope, without being too sanguine; for we must bear in mind that humanity has yet by no means emerged from the period of "sacrificed generations." History has known no others; and it is possible that, to the end of time, all generations may call themselves sacrificed. Nevertheless, it cannot be denied that the sacrifices, however unjust and useless they still may be, are growing ever less inhuman and less inevitable; and that the laws which govern them are becoming better and better known, and would seem to draw nearer and nearer to those that a lofty mind might accept without being pitiless.

32

It must be admitted, however, that a majestic, redoubtable slowness attends the movements of these "ideas of the species." Centuries had to pass before it dawned upon primitive men, who fled from each other, or fought when they met at the mouth of their caverns, that they would do well to form into groups, and unite in defence against the mighty enemies who threatened them from without. And besides, these "ideas" of the species will often be widely different from those that the wisest man might hold. They would seem to be independent, spontaneous, often based on facts of which no trace is shown by the human reason of the epoch that witnessed their birth; and indeed there is no graver or more disturbing problem before the moralist or sociologist than that of determining whether all his efforts can hasten by one hour or divert by one hair's-breadth the decisions of the great anonymous mass which proceeds, step by step, towards its indiscernible goal.

Long ago—so long indeed that this is one of the first affirmations of science when, quitting the bowels of the earth, the glaciers and grottoes, it ceased to call itself geology and palaeontology and became the history of man—humanity passed through a crisis not wholly unlike that which now lies ahead of it, or is actually menacing it at the moment; the difference being only that in those days the dilemma seemed vastly more tragic and more unsolvable. It may truly be said that mankind never has known a more perilous or more decisive hour, or a period when it drew nearer its ruin; and the fact that we exist to-day would appear to be due to the unexpected expedient which saved the race at the moment when the scourge that fed on man's very reason, on all that was best and most irresistible in his instinct of justice and injustice, was actually on the point of destroying the heroic equilibrium between the desire to live and the possibility of living.

I refer to the acts of violence, rapine, outrage, murder, which were of natural occurrence among the earliest human groups. These crimes, which will probably have been of the most frightful description, must have very seriously endangered the existence of the race; for vengeance is the terrible, and, as it were, the epidemic form which the craving for justice at first assumes. Now this spirit of vengeance, abandoned to itself and forever multiplying—revenge followed by the revenge of revenge—would finally have engulfed, if not the whole of mankind, at least all those of the earliest men who were possessed of energy or pride. We find, however, that among these barbarous races, as among most of the existing savage tribes whose habits are known to us, there comes a time, usually at the period when their weapons are growing too deadly, when this vengeance suddenly halts before a singular custom, known as the "blood-tribute," or the "composition for murder;" which allows the homicide to escape the reprisals of the victim's friends and relations by payment to them of an indemnity, that, from being arbitrary at the start, soon becomes strictly graduated.

In the whole history of these infant races, in whom impulse and heroism were the predominant factors, there is nothing stranger, nothing more astounding, than this almost universal custom, which for all its ingenuity would seem almost too long-suffering and mercantile. May we attribute it to the foresight of the chiefs? We find it in races among whom authority might almost be said to be entirely lacking. Did it originate among the old men, the thinkers, the sages, of the primitive groups? That is not more probable. For underlying this custom there is a thought which is at the same time higher and lower than could be the thought of an isolated prophet or genius of those barbarous days. The sage, the prophet, the genius—above all, the untrained genius—is rather inclined to carry to extremes the generous and heroic tendencies of the clan or epoch to which he belongs. He would have recoiled in disgust from this timid, cunning evasion of a natural and sacred revenge, from this odious traffic in friendship, fidelity, and love. Nor is it conceivable, on the other hand, that he should have attained sufficient loftiness of spirit to be able to let his gaze travel beyond the noblest and most incontestable duties of the moment, and to behold only the superior interest of the tribe or the race: that mysterious desire for life, which the wisest of the wise among us to-day are generally unable to perceive or to justify until they have wrought grave and painful conquest over their isolated reason and their heart.

No, it was not the thought of man which found the solution. On the contrary, it was the unconsciousness of the mass, compelled to act in self-defence against thoughts too intrinsically, individually human to satisfy the irreducible exigencies of life on this earth. The species is extremely patient, extremely long-suffering. It will bear as long as it can and carry as far as it can the burden which reason, the desire for improvement, the imagination, the passions, vices, virtues, and feelings natural to man, may combine to impose upon it. But the moment the burden becomes too overwhelming, and disaster threatens, the species will instantaneously, with the utmost indifference, fling it aside. It is careless as to the means; it will adopt the one that is nearest, the simplest, most practical, being doubtless perfectly satisfied that its own idea is the justest and best. And of ideas it has only one, which is that it wishes to live; and truly this idea surpasses all the heroism, all the generous dreams, that may have reposed in the burden which it has discarded.

And indeed, in the history of human reason, the greatest and the justest thoughts are not always those which attain the loftiest heights. It happens somewhat with the thoughts of men as with a fountain; for it is only because the water has been imprisoned and escapes through a narrow opening that it soars so proudly into the air. As it issues from this opening and hurls itself towards the sky, it would seem to despise the great, illimitable, motionless lake that stretches out far beneath it. And yet, say what one will, it is the lake that is right. For all its apparent motionlessness, for all its silence, it is tranquilly accomplishing the immense and normal task of the most important element of our globe; and the jet of water is merely a curious incident, which soon returns into the universal scheme. To us the species is the great, unerring lake; and this even from the point of view of the superior human reason that it would seem at times to offend. Its idea is the vastest of all, and contains every other; it embraces limitless time and space. And does not each day that goes by reveal more and more clearly to us that the vastest idea, no matter where it reside, always ends by becoming the most just and most reasonable, the wisest and the most beautiful?

33

There are times when we ask ourselves whether it might not be well for humanity that its destinies should be governed by the superior men among us, the great sages, rather than by the instinct of the species, that is always so slow and often so cruel.

It is doubtful whether this question could be answered to-day in quite the same fashion as formerly. It would surely have been highly dangerous to confide the destinies of the species to Plato or Aristotle, Marcus Aurelius, Shakespeare, or Montesquieu. At the very worst moments of the French Revolution the fate of the people was in the hands of philosophers of none too mean an order. It cannot be denied, however, that in our time the habits of the thinker have undergone a great change. He has ceased to be speculative or Utopian; he is no longer exclusively intuitive. In politics as in literature, in philosophy as in all the sciences, he displays less imagination, but his powers as an observer have grown. He inclines rather to concentrate his attention on the thing that is, to study it and strive at its organisation, than to precede it, or to endeavour to create what is not yet, or never shall be. And therefore he may possibly have some claim to more authoritative utterance; nor would so much danger attend his more direct intervention. It must be admitted, however, that there is no greater likelihood now than in former times of such intervention being permitted him. Nay, there is less, perhaps; for having become more circumspect and less blinded by narrow convictions, he will be less audacious, less imperious, and less impatient. And yet it is possible that, finding himself in natural sympathy with the species which he is content merely to observe, he will by slow degrees acquire more and more influence; so that here again, in ultimate analysis, it is the species that will be right, the species that will decide: for it will have guided him who observes it, and therefore, in following him whom it has guided, it will truly only be following its own unconscious, formless desires, which shall have been expressed by him, and by him brought into light.

34

Until such time as the species shall discover the new and needful experiment—and this it will quickly do when the danger becomes more acute; nay, for all we know, the expedient may have already been found, and, entirely unsuspected of us, be already transforming part of our destinies—until such time, while bound to act in external matters as though our brothers' salvation depended entirely on our exertions, it is open to us, no less than to the sages of old, to retire occasionally within ourselves. We in our turn shall perhaps find there "one of those things" of which the contemplation shall suffice to bring us instantaneous enjoyment, if not of the perfect calm, at least of an indestructible hope. Though nature appear unjust, though nothing authorise us to declare that a superior power, or the intellect of the universe, rewards or punishes, here below or elsewhere, in accordance with the laws of our consciousness or with other laws that we shall some day admit; and, finally, though between man and man, in other words, in our relations with our fellows, our admirable desire for equity translate itself into a justice that is always incomplete, at the mercy of every error of reason, of every ambush laid by personal interest, and of all the evil habits of a social condition that still is sub-human, it is none the less certain that an image of that invisible and incorruptible justice, which we have vainly sought in the sky or the universe, reposes in the depths of the moral life of every man. And though its method of action be such as to cause it to pass unperceived of most of our fellows, often even of our own consciousness, though all that it does be hidden and intangible, it is none the less profoundly human and profoundly real. It would seem to hear, to examine, all that we say and think and strive for in our exterior life; and if it find a little sincerity beneath, a little earnest desire for good, it will transform these into moral forces that shall extend and illumine our inner life, and help us to better thoughts, better speech, better endeavour in the time to come. It will not add to, or take from, our wealth; it will bring no immunity from disease or from lightning; it will not prolong by one hour the life of the being we cherish; but if we have learned to reflect and to love, if, in other words, heart and brain have both done their duty, it will establish in heart and brain a contentment that, though perhaps stripped of illusion, shall still be inexhaustible and noble; it will confer a dignity of existence, and an intelligence, that shall suffice to sustain our life after the loss of our wealth, after the stroke of disease or of lightning has fallen, after the loved one has for ever quitted our arms. A good thought or deed brings a reward to our heart that it cannot, in the absence of an universal judge of nature, extend to the things around. It endeavours to create within us the happiness it is unable to produce in our material life. Denied all external outlet, it fills our soul the more. It prepares the space that soon shall be required by our developing intellect, our expanding peace and love. Helpless against the laws of nature, it is all-powerful over those that govern the happy equilibrium of human consciousness. And this is true of every stage of thought, of every class of action. A vast distance might seem to divide the labourer who brings up his children honourably, lives his humble life and honourably does the work that falls to his lot, from the man who steadfastly perseveres in moral heroism; but each of these is acting and living on the same plane as the other, and the same loyal, consoling region receives them both. And though it be certain that what we say and do must largely influence our material happiness, yet, in ultimate analysis, it is only by means of the spiritual organs that even material happiness can be fully and permanently enjoyed. Hence the preponderating importance of thought. But of supreme importance, from the point of view of the reception we shall offer to the joys and sorrows of life, is the character, the frame of mind, the moral condition, that the things we have said and done and thought will have created within us. Here is evidence of admirable justice; and the intimate happiness that our moral being derives from the constant striving of the mind and heart for good, becomes the more comprehensible when we realise that this happiness is only the surface of the goodly thought or feeling that is shining within our heart. Here may we indeed find that intelligent, moral bond between cause and effect that we have vainly sought in the external world; here, in moral matters, reigning over the good and evil that are warring in the depths of our consciousness, may we in truth discover a justice exactly similar to the one which we could desire to recognise in physical matters. But whence do we derive this desire if not from the justice within us; and is it not because this justice is so mighty and active in our heart that we are reluctant to believe in its non-existence in the universe?

35

We have spoken at great length of justice; but is it not the great mystery of man, the one that tends to take the place of most of the spiritual mysteries that govern his destiny? It has dethroned more than one god, more than one nameless power. It is the star evolved from the nebulous mass of our instincts and our incomprehensible life. It is not the word of the enigma; and when, in the fulness of time, it shall become clearer to us, and shall truly reign all over the earth, there will come to us no greater knowledge of what we are, or why we are, whence we come or whither we go; but we shall at least have obeyed the first word of the enigma, and shall proceed, with a freer spirit and a more tranquil heart, to the search for its last secret.

Finally, it comprises all the human virtues; and none but itself can offer the welcoming smile whereby these are ennobled and purified, none but itself can accord them the right to penetrate deep into our moral life. For every virtue must be maleficent and steeped in artifice that cannot support the fixed and eager regard of justice. And so do we find it too at the heart of our every ideal. It is at the centre of our love of truth, at the centre of our love of beauty. It is kindness and pity, it is generosity, heroism, love; for all these are the acts of justice of one who has risen sufficiently high to perceive that justice and injustice are not exclusively confined to what lies before him, to the narrow circle of obligations chance may have imposed, but that they stretch far beyond years, beyond neighbouring destinies, beyond what he regards as his duty, beyond what he loves, beyond what he seeks and encounters, beyond what he approves or rejects, beyond his doubts and his fears, beyond the wrong-doing and even the crimes of the men, his brothers.

Maurice Maeterlinck

II

THE EVOLUTION OF MYSTERY

1

It is not unreasonable to believe that the paramount interest of life, all that is truly lofty and remarkable in the destiny of man, reposes almost entirely in the mystery that surrounds us; in the two mysteries, it may be, that are mightiest, most dreadful of all—fatality and death. And indeed there are many whom the fatigue induced in their minds by the natural uncertainties of science has almost compelled to accept this belief. I too believe, though in a somewhat different fashion, that the study of mystery in all its forms is the noblest to which the mind of man can devote itself; and truly it has ever been the occupation and care of those who in science and art, in philosophy and literature, have refused to be satisfied merely to observe and portray the trivial, well-recognised truths, facts, and realities of life. And we find that the success of these men in their endeavour, the depth of their insight into all that they know, has most strictly accorded with the respect in which they held all they did not know, with the dignity that their mind or imagination was able to confer on the sum of unknowable forces. Our consciousness of the unknown wherein we have being gives life a meaning and grandeur which must of necessity be absent if we persist in considering only the things that are known to us; if we too readily incline to believe that these must greatly transcend in importance the things that we know not yet.

2

It behoves every man to frame for himself his own general conception of the world. On this conception reposes his whole human and moral existence. But this general conception of the world, when closely examined, is truly no more than a general conception of the unknown. And we must be careful; we have not the right, when ideas so vast confront us, ideas the results of which are so highly important, to select the one which seems most magnificent to us, most beautiful, or most attractive. The duty lies on us to choose the idea which seems truest, or rather the only one which seems true; for I decline to believe that we can sincerely hesitate between the truth that is only apparent and the one that is real. The moment must always come when we feel that one of these two is possessed of more truth than the other. And to this truth we should cling: in our actions, our words, and our thoughts; in our art, in our science, in the life of our feelings and intellect. Its definition, perhaps, may elude us. It may possibly bring not one grain of reassuring conviction. Nay, essentially, perhaps, it may be but the merest impression, though profounder and more sincere than any previous impression. These things do not matter. It is not imperative that the truth we have chosen should be unimpeachable or of absolute certainty. There is already great gain in our having been brought to experience that the truths we had loved before did not accord with reality or with faithful experience of life; and we have every reason, therefore, to cherish our truth with heartiest gratitude until its own turn shall come to experience the fate it inflicted on its predecessor. The great mischief, the one which destroys our moral existence and threatens the integrity of our mind and our character, is not that we should deceive ourselves and love an uncertain truth, but that we should remain constant to one in which we no longer wholly believe.

3

If we sought nothing more than to invest our conception of the unknown with the utmost possible grandeur and tragedy, magnificence and might, there would be no need of such restrictions. From many points of view, doubtless, the most beautiful, most touching, most religious attitude in face of mystery is silence, and prayer, and fearful acceptance. When this immense, irresistible force confronts us—this inscrutable, ceaselessly vigilant power, humanly super-human, sovereignly intelligent, and, for all we know, even personal —must it not, at first sight, seem more reverent, worthier, to offer complete submission, trying only to master our terror, than tranquilly to set on foot a patient, laborious investigation? But is the choice possible to us; have we still the right to choose? The beauty or dignity of the attitude we shall assume no longer is matter of moment. It is truth and sincerity that are called for to-day for the facing of all things—how much more when mystery confronts us! In the past, the prostration of man, his bending the knee, seemed beautiful because of what, in the past, seemed to be true. We have acquired no fresh certitude, perhaps; but for us, none the less, the truth of the past has ceased to be true. We have not bridged the unknown; but still, though we know not what it is, we do partially know what it is not; and it is before this we should bow, were the attitude of our fathers to be once more assumed by us. For although it has not, perhaps, been incontrovertibly proved that the unknown is neither vigilant nor personal, neither sovereignly intelligent nor sovereignly just, or that it possesses none of the passions, intentions, virtues and vices of man, it is still incomparably more probable that the unknown is entirely indifferent to all that appears of supreme importance in this life of ours. It is incomparably more probable that if, in the vast and eternal scheme of the unknown, a minute and ephemeral place be reserved for man, his actions, be he the strongest or weakest, the best or the worst of men, will be as unimportant there as the movements of the obscurest geological cell in the history of ocean or continent. Though it may not have been irrefutably shown that the infinite and invisible are not for ever hovering round us, dealing out sorrow or joy in accordance with our good or evil intentions, guiding our destiny step by step, and preparing, with the help of innumerable forces, the incomprehensible but eternal law that governs the accidents of our birth, our future, our death, and our life beyond the tomb, it is still incomparably more probable that the invisible and infinite, intervene as they may at every moment in our life, enter therein only as stupendous, blind, indifferent elements; and that though they pass over us, in us, penetrate into our being, and inspire and mould our life, they are as careless of our individual existence as air, water, or light. And the whole of our conscious life, the life that forms our one certitude, that is our one fixed point in time and space, rests upon "incomparable probabilities" of this nature; but rarely are they as "incomparable" as these.

4

The hour when a lofty conviction forsakes us should never be one of regret. If a belief we have clung to goes, or a spring snaps within us; if we at last dethrone the idea that so long has held sway, this is proof of vitality, progress, of our marching steadily onwards, and making good use of all that lies to our hand. We should rejoice at the knowledge that the thought which so long has sustained us is proved incapable

Maurice Maeterlinck

now of even sustaining itself. And though we have nothing to put in the place of the spring that lies broken, there need still be no cause for sadness. Far better the place remain empty than that it be filled by a spring which the rust corrodes, or by a new truth in which we do not wholly believe. And besides, the place is not really empty. Determinate truth may not yet have arrived, but still, in its own deep recess, there hides a truth without name, which waits and calls. And if it wait and call too long in the void, and nothing arise in the place of the vanished spring, it still shall be found that, in moral no less than in physical life, necessity will be able to create the organ it needs, and that the negative truth will at last find sufficient force in itself to set the idle machinery going. And the lives that possess no more than one force of this kind are not the least strenuous, the least ardent, or the least useful.

And even though our belief forsake us entirely, it still will take with it nothing of what we have given, nor will there be lost one single sincere, religious, disinterested effort that we have put forth to ennoble this faith, to exalt or embellish it. Every thought we have added, each worthy sacrifice we have had the courage to make in its name, will have left its indelible mark on our moral existence. The body is gone, but the palace it built still stands, and the space it has conquered will remain for ever unenclosed. It is our duty, and one we dare not renounce, to prepare homes for truths that shall come, to maintain in good order the forces destined to serve them, and to create open spaces within us; nor can the time thus employed be possibly wasted.

5

These thoughts have arisen within me through my having been compelled, a few days ago, to glance through two or three little dramas of mine, wherein lies revealed the disquiet of a mind that has given itself wholly to mystery; a disquiet legitimate enough in itself, perhaps, but not so inevitable as to warrant its own complacency. The keynote of these little plays is dread of the unknown that surrounds us. I, or rather some obscure poetical feeling within me (for with the sincerest of poets a division must often be made between the instinctive feeling of their art and the thoughts of their real life), seemed to believe in a species of monstrous, invisible, fatal power that gave heed to our every action, and was hostile to our smile, to our life, to our peace and our love. Its intentions could not be divined, but the spirit of the drama assumed them to be malevolent always. In its essence, perhaps, this power was just, but only in anger; and it exercised justice in a manner so crooked, so secret, so sluggish and remote, that its punishments—for it never rewarded—took the semblance of inexplicable, arbitrary acts of fate. We had there, in a word, more or less the idea of the God of the Christian blent with that of ancient fatality, lurking in nature's impenetrable twilight, whence it eagerly watched, contested, and saddened the projects, the feelings, the thoughts and the happiness of man.

6

This unknown would most frequently appear in the shape of death. The presence of death—infinite, menacing, for ever treacherously active—filled every interstice of the poem. The problem of existence was answered only by the enigma of annihilation. And it was a callous, inexorable death; blind, and groping its mysterious way with only chance to guide it; laying its hands preferentially on the youngest and the least unhappy, since these held themselves less motionless than others, and that every too sudden movement in the night arrested its attention. And around it were only poor little trembling, elementary creatures, who shivered for an instant and wept, on the brink of a gulf; and their words and their tears had importance only from the fact that each word they spoke and each tear they shed fell into this gulf, and were at times so strangely resonant there as to lead one to think that the gulf must be vast if tear or word, as it fell, could send forth so confused and muffled a sound.

7

Such a conception of life is not healthy, whatever show of reason it may seem to possess; and I would not allude to it here were it not for the fact that we find this idea, or one closely akin to it, governing the hearts of most men, however tranquil, or thoughtful, or earnest they may be, at the approach of the slightest misfortune. There is evidently a side to our nature which, notwithstanding all we may learn and master and the certitudes we may acquire, destines us never to be other than poor, weak, useless creatures, consecrated to death, and playthings of the vast and indifferent forces that surround us. We appear for an instant in limitless space, our one appreciable mission the propagation of a species that itself has no appreciable mission in the scheme of a universe whose extent and duration baffle the most daring, most powerful brain. This is a truth; it is one of those profound but sterile truths which the poet may salute as he passes on his way; but it is a truth in the neighbourhood of which the man with the thousand duties who lives in the poet will do well not to abide too long. And of truths such as this many are lofty and deserving of all our respect, but in their domain it were unwise to lay ourselves down and sleep. So many truths environ us that it may safely be said that few men can be found, of the wickedest even, who have not for counsel and guide a grave and respectable truth. Yes, it is a truth—the vastest, most certain of truths, if one will—that our life is nothing, and our efforts the merest jest; our existence, that of our planet, only a miserable accident in the history of worlds; but it is no less a truth that, to us, our life and our planet are the most important, nay, the only important phenomena in the history of worlds. And of these truths which is the truer? Does the first of necessity destroy the second? Without the second, should we have had the courage to formulate the first? The one appeals to our imagination, and may be helpful to it in its own domain; but the other directly interests our actual life. It is well that each have its share. The truth that is undoubtedly truest from the human point of view must evidently appeal to us more than the truth which is truest from the universal point of view. Ignorant as we are of the aim of the universe, how shall we tell whether or no it concern itself with the interests of our race? The probable futility of our life and our species is a truth which regards us indirectly only, and may well, therefore, be left in suspense. The other truth, that indicates clearly the importance of life, may perhaps be more restricted, but it has a direct, incontestable, actual bearing upon ourselves. To sacrifice or even subordinate it to an alien truth must surely be wrong. The first truth should never be lost sight of; it will strengthen and illumine the second, whose government will thus become more intelligent and benign: the first truth will teach us to profit by all that the second does not include. And if we allow it to sadden our heart or arrest our action, we have not sufficiently realised that the vast but precarious space it fills in the region of important truths is governed by countless problems which as yet are unsolved; while the problems whereon the second truth rests are daily resolved by real life. The first truth is still in the dangerous, feverish stage, through which all truths must pass before they can penetrate freely into our heart and our brain; a stage of jealousy, truculence, which renders the neighbourhood of another truth insupportable to them. We must wait till the fever subsides; and if the home that we have prepared in our spirit be sufficiently spacious and lofty, we shall find very soon that the most contradictory truths will be conscious only of the mysterious bond that unites them, and will silently join with each other to place in the front rank of all, and there help and sustain, that truth from among them which calmly went on with its work while the others were fretfully jangling; that truth which can do the most good, and brings with it the uttermost hope.

The strangest feature of the present time is the confusion which reigns in our instincts and feelings—in our ideas, too, save at our most lucid, most tranquil, most thoughtful moments—on the subject of the intervention of the unknown or mysterious in the truly grave events of life. We find, amidst this confusion, feelings which no longer accord with any precise, living, accepted idea; such, for instance, as concern the existence of a determinate God, conceived as more or less anthropomorphic, providential, personal, and unceasingly vigilant. We find feelings which, as yet, are only partially ideas; as those which deal with fatality, destiny, the justice of things. We find ideas which will soon turn into feelings; those that treat of the law of the species, evolution, selection, the will-power of the race, &c. And, finally, we discover ideas which still are purely ideas, too uncertain and scattered for us to be able to predict at what moment they will become feelings, and thus materially influence our actions, our acceptance of life, our joys, and our sorrows.

9

If in actual life this confusion is not so apparent, it is only because actual life will but rarely express itself, or condescend to make use of image or formula to relate its experience. This state of mind, however, is clearly discernible in all those whose self-imposed mission it is to depict real life, to explain and interpret it, and throw light on the hidden causes of good and evil destiny. It is of the poets I speak, of dramatic poets above all, who are occupied with external and active life; and it matters not whether they produce novels, tragedies, the drama properly so called, or historical studies, for I give to the words poets and dramatic poets their widest significance.

It cannot be denied that the possession of a dominant idea, one that may be said to exclude all others, must confer considerable power on the poet, or "interpreter of life;" and in the degree that the idea is mysterious, and difficult of definition or control, will be the extent of this power and its conspicuousness in the poem. And this is entirely legitimate, so long as the poet himself has not the least doubt as to the value of his idea; and there are many admirable poets who have never hesitated, paused, or doubted. Thus it is that we find the idea of heroic duty filling so enormous a space in the tragedies of Corneille, that of absolute faith in the dramas of Calderon, that of the tyranny of destiny in the works of Sophocles.

10

Of these three ideas, that of heroic duty is the most human and the least mysterious; and although far more restricted to-day than at the time of Corneille—for there are few such duties which it would not now be reasonable, and even heroic, perhaps, to call into question, and it becomes ever more and more difficult to find one that is truly heroic—conditions may still be imagined under which recourse thereto may be legitimate in the poet.

But will he discover in faith—to-day no more than a shadowy memory to the most fervent believer—that inspiration and strength, by whose aid Corneille was able to depict the God of the Christians as the august, omnipresent actor of his dramas, invisible but untiringly active, and sovereign always? Or is it possible still for a reasonable being, whose eyes rest calmly on the life about him, to believe in the tyranny of fate; of that sluggish, unswerving, preordained, inscrutable force which urges a given man, or family, by given ways to a given disaster or death? For though it be true that our life is subject to many an unknown force, we at least are aware that these forces would seem to be blind, indifferent, unconscious, and that their most insidious attacks may be in some measure averted by the wisest among us. Can we still be allowed, then, to believe that the universe holds a power so idle, so wretched, as to concern itself solely in saddening, frustrating, and terrifying the projects and schemes of man?

Immanent justice is another mysterious and sovereign force, whereof use has been made; but it is only the feeblest of writers who have ventured to accept this postulate in its entirety: only those to whom reality and probability were matters of smallest moment. The affirmation that wickedness is necessarily and visibly punished in this life, and virtue as necessarily and visibly rewarded, is too manifestly opposed to the most elementary daily experience, too wildly inconsistent a dream, for the true poet ever to accept it as the basis of his drama. And, on the other hand, if we refer to a future life the bestowal of reward and punishment, we are merely entering by another gate the region of divine justice. For, indeed, unless immanent justice be infallible, permanent, unvarying, and inevitable, it becomes no more than a curious, well-meaning caprice of fate; and from that moment it no longer is justice, or even fate: it shrinks into merest chance—in other words, almost into nothingness.

There is, it is true, a very real immanent justice; I refer to the force which enacts that the vicious, malevolent, cruel, disloyal man shall be morally less happy than he who is honest and good, affectionate, gentle, and just. But here it is inward justice whose workings we see; a very human, natural, comprehensible force, the study of whose cause and effect must of necessity lead to psychological drama, where there no longer is need of the vast and mysterious background which lent its solemn and awful perspective to the events of history and legend. But is it legitimate deliberately to misconceive the unknown that governs our life in order that we may reconstruct this mysterious background?

11

While on this subject of dominant and mysterious ideas, we shall do well to consider the forms that the idea of fatality has taken, and for ever is taking: for fatality even to-day still provides the supreme explanation for all that we cannot explain; and it is to fatality still that the thoughts of the "interpreter of life" unceasingly turn.

The poets have endeavoured to transform it, to make it attractive, to restore its youth. They have contrived, in their works, a hundred new and winding canals through which they may introduce the icy waters of the great and desolate river whose banks have been gradually shunned by the dwellings of men. And of those most successful in making us share the illusion that they were conferring a solemn, definitive meaning on life, there are few who have not instinctively recognised the sovereign importance conferred on the actions of men by the irresponsible power of an ever august and unerring destiny. Fatality would seem to be the pre-eminent tragical force; it no sooner appears in a drama than it does of itself three-fourths of all that needs doing. It may safely be said that the poet who could find to-day, in material science, in the unknown that surrounds us, or in his own heart, the equivalent for ancient fatality—a force, that is, of equally irresistible predestination, a force as universally admitted—would infallibly produce a masterpiece. It is true, however, that he would have, at the same time, to solve the mighty enigma for whose word we are all of us seeking, so that this supposition is not likely to be realised very soon.

12

This is the source, then, whence the lustral water is drawn with which the poets have purified the cruellest of tragedies. There is an instinct in man that worships fatality, and he is apt to regard whatever pertains thereto as incontestable, solemn, and beautiful. His cry is for freedom; but circumstances arise when he rather would tell himself that he is not free. The unbending, malignant goddess is more acceptable often than the divinity who only asks for an effort that shall avert disaster. All things notwithstanding, it pleases us still to be ruled by a power that nothing can turn from its purpose; and whatever our mental dignity may lose by such a belief is gained by a kind of sentimental vanity in us, which complacently dwells on the measureless force that for ever keeps watch on our plans, and confers on our simplest action a mysterious, eternal significance. Fatality, briefly, explains and excuses all things, by relegating to a sufficient distance in the invisible or the unintelligible all that it would be hard to explain, and more difficult still to excuse.

13

Therefore it is that so many have turned to the dismembered

statue of the terrible goddess who reigned in the dramas of Euripides, Sophocles, and Aeschylus, and that the scattered fragments of her limbs have provided more than one poet with the marble required for the fashioning of a newer divinity, who should be more human, less arbitrary, and less inconceivable than she of old. The fatality of the passions, for instance, has thus been evolved. But for a passion truly to be fatal in a soul aware of itself, for the mystery to reappear that shall make crime pardonable by investing it with loftiness and lifting it high above the will of man: for these we require the intervention of a God, or some other equally irresistible, infinite force. Wagner, therefore, in "Tristram and Iseult," makes use of the philtre, as Shakespeare of the witches in "Macbeth," Racine of the oracle of Calchas in "Iphigenia" and of Venus' hatred in "Phedre." We have travelled in a circle, and find ourselves back once more at the very heart of the craving of former days. This expedient may be more or less legitimate in archaic or legendary drama, where there is room for all kinds of poetic fantasy; but in the drama which pretends to actual truth we demand another intervention, one that shall seem to us more genuinely irresistible, if crimes like Macbeth's, such a deed of horror as that to which Agamemnon consented: perhaps, too, the kind of love that burned in Phedre, shall achieve their mysterious excuse, and acquire a grandeur and sombre nobility that intrinsically they do not possess. Take away from Macbeth the fatal predestination, the intervention of hell, the heroic struggle with an occult justice that for ever is revealing itself through a thousand fissures of revolting nature, and Macbeth is merely a frantic, contemptible murderer. Take away the oracle of Calchas, and Agamemnon becomes abominable. Take away the hatred of Venus, and what is Phedre but a neurotic creature, whose "moral quality" and power of resistance to evil are too pronouncedly feeble for our intellect to take any genuine interest in the calamity that befalls her?

14

The truth is that these supernatural interventions to-day satisfy neither spectator nor reader. Though he know it not, perhaps, and strive as he may, it is no longer possible for him to regard them seriously in the depths of his consciousness. His conception of the universe is other. He no longer detects the working of a narrow, determined, obstinate, violent will in the multitude of forces that strive in him and about him. He knows that the criminal whom he may meet in actual life has been urged into crime by misfortune, education, atavism, or by movements of passion which he has himself experienced and subdued, while recognising that there might have been circumstances under which their repression would have been a matter of exceeding difficulty. He will not, it is true, always be able to discover the cause of these misfortunes or movements of passion; and his endeavour to account for the injustice of education or heredity will probably be no less unsuccessful. But, for all that, he will no longer incline to attribute a particular crime to the wrath of a God, the direct intervention of hell, or to a series of changeless decrees inscribed in the book of fate. Why ask of him, then, to accept in a poem an explanation which he refuses in life? Is the poet's duty not rather to furnish an explanation loftier, clearer, more widely and profoundly human than any his reader can find for himself? For, indeed, this wrath of the gods, intervention of hell, and writing in letters of fire, are to him no more to-day than so many symbols that have long ceased to content him. It is time that the poet should realise that the symbol is legitimate only when it stands for accepted truth, or for truth which as yet we cannot, or will not, accept; but the symbol is out of place at a time when it is truth itself that we seek. And, besides, to merit admission into a really living poem, the symbol should be at least as great and beautiful as the truth for which it stands, and should, moreover, precede this truth, and not follow a long way behind.

15

We see, therefore, how surpassingly difficult it must have become to introduce great crimes, or cruel, unbridled, tragical passions, into a modern work, above all if that work be destined for stage presentation; for the poet will seek in vain for the mysterious excuse these crimes or passions demand. And yet, for all that, so deeply is this craving for mysterious excuse implanted within us, so satisfied are we that man is, at bottom, never as guilty as he may appear to be, that we are still fully content, when considering passions or crimes of this nature, to admit some kind of fatal intervention that at least may not seem too manifestly unacceptable.

This excuse, however, will be sought by us only when the persons guilty of crimes which are contrary to human nature, when the victims of misfortunes which they could not foresee, and which seem undeserved to us, inexplicable, wholly abnormal, are more or less superior beings, possessed of their fullest share of consciousness. We are loath to admit that an extraordinary crime or disaster can have a purely human cause. In spite of all, we persistently seek in some way to explain the inexplicable. We should not be satisfied if the poet were simply to say to us: "You see here the wrong that was done by this strong, this conscious, intelligent man. Behold the misfortune this hero encountered; this good man's ruin and sorrow. See, too, how this sage is crushed by tragic, irremediable wickedness. The human causes of these events are evident to you. I have no other explanation to offer, unless it be perhaps the indifference of the universe towards the actions of man." Our dissatisfaction would vanish if he could succeed in conveying to us the sensation of this

Maurice Maeterlinck

indifference, if he could show it in action; but, as it is the property of indifference never to interfere or act, that would seem to be more or less unachievable.

16

But when we turn to the by no means inevitable jealousy of Othello, or to the misfortunes of Romeo and Juliet, which were surely not preordained, we discover no need of explanation, or of the purifying influence of fatality. In another drama, Ford's masterpiece, "'Tis Pity She's a Whore," which revolves around the incestuous love of Giovanni for his sister Annabella, we are compelled either to turn away in horror, or to seek the mysterious excuse in its habitual haunt on the shore of the gulf. But even here, the first painful shock over, we find it is not imperative. For the love of brother for sister, viewed from a standpoint sufficiently lofty, is a crime against morality, but not against human nature; and there is at least some measure of palliation in the youth of the pair, and in the passion that blinds them. Othello, too, the semi-barbarian who does Desdemona to death, has been goaded to madness by the machinations of Iago; and even this last can plead his by no means gratuitous hatred. The disasters that weighed so heavily on the lovers of Verona were due to the inexperience of the victims, to the manifest disproportion between their strength and that of their enemies; and although we may pity the man who succumbs to superior human force, his downfall does not surprise us. We are not impelled to seek explanation elsewhere, to ask questions of fate; and unless he appear to fall victim to superhuman injustice, we are content to tell ourselves that what has happened was bound to happen. It is only when disaster occurs after every precaution is taken that we could ourselves have devised, that we become conscious of the need for other explanation.

We find it difficult, therefore, to conceive or admit as naturally, humanly possible that a crime shall be committed by a person who apparently is endowed with fullest intelligence and consciousness; or that misfortune should befall him which seems in its essence to be inexplicable, undeserved, and unexpected. It follows, therefore, that the poet can only place on the stage (this phrase I use merely as an abbreviation: it would be more correct to say, "cause us to assist at some adventure whereof we know personally neither the actors nor the totality of the circumstances") faults, crimes, and acts of injustice committed by persons of defective consciousness, as also disasters befalling feeble beings unable to control their desires—innocent creatures, it may be, but thick-sighted, imprudent, and reckless. Under these conditions there would seem to be no call for the intervention of anything beyond the limit of normal human psychology. But such a conception of the theatre would be at absolute variance with real life, where we find crimes committed by persons of fullest consciousness, and the most inexplicable, inconceivable, unmerited misfortunes befalling the wisest, the best, most virtuous and prudent of men. Dramas which deal with unconscious creatures, whom their own feebleness oppresses and their own desires overcome, excite our interest and arouse our pity; but the veritable drama, the one which probes to the heart of things and grapples with important truths—our own personal drama, in a word, which for ever hangs over our life—is the one wherein the strong, intelligent, and conscious commit errors, faults, and crimes which are almost inevitable; wherein the wise and upright struggle with all-powerful calamity, with forces destructive to wisdom and virtue: for it is worthy of note that the spectator, however feeble, dishonest even, he may be in real life, still enrols himself always among the virtuous, just, and strong; and when he reflects on the misfortunes of the weak, or even witnesses them, he resolutely declines to imagine himself in the place of the victims.

18

Here we attain the limit of the human will, the gloomy boundary-line of the influence that the most just and enlightened of men is able to exert on events that decide his future happiness or sorrow. No great drama exists, or poem of lofty aim, but one of its heroes shall stray to this frontier where his destiny waits for the seal. Why has this wise, this virtuous man committed this fault or this crime? Why has that woman, who knows so well the meaning of all that she does, hazarded the gesture which must so inevitably summon everlasting sorrow? By whom have the links been forged of the chain of disaster whose fetters have crushed this innocent family? Why do all things crumble around one, and fall into ruins, while the other, his neighbour, less active and strong, less skilful and wise, finds ever material by him to build up his life anew? Why do tenderness, beauty, and love flock to the path of some, where others meet hatred only, and malice, and treachery? Why persistent happiness here, and yonder, though merits be equal, nought but unceasing disaster? Why is this house for ever beset with the storm, while over that other there shines the peace of unvarying stars? Why genius, and riches, and health on this side, and yonder disease, imbecility, poverty? Whence has the passion been sent that has wrought such terrible grief, and whence the passion that proved the source of such wonderful joy? Why does the youth whom yesterday I met go on his tranquil road to profoundest happiness, while his friend, with the same methodical, peaceful, ignorant step, proceeds on his way to death?

19

Life will often place such problems before us; but how rarely are we compelled to refer their solution to the supernatural, mysterious, superhuman, or preordained! It is only the fervent believer who will still be content to see there the finger of divine intervention. Such of us, however, as have entered the house where the storm has raged, as well as the house of peace, have rarely departed without most clearly detecting the essentially human reasons of both peace and storm. We who have known the wise and upright man who has been guilty of error or crime, are acquainted also with the circumstances which induced his action, and these circumstances seem to us in no way supernatural. As we draw near to the woman whose gesture brought misery to her, we learn very soon that this gesture might have been avoided, and that, in her place, we should have refrained. The friends of the man around whom all fell into ruins, and of the neighbour who ever was able to build up his life anew, will have observed before that the acorn sometimes will fall on to rock, and sometimes on fertile soil. And though poverty, sickness, and death still remain the three inequitable goddesses of human existence, they no longer awake in us the superstitious fears of bygone days We regard them to-day as essentially indifferent, unconscious, blind. We know that they recognise none of the ideal laws which we once believed that they sanctioned; and it only too often has happened that at the very moment we were whispering to ourselves of "purification, trial, reward, punishment," their undiscerning caprice gave the lie to the too lofty, too moral title which we were about to bestow.

20

Our imagination, it is true, is inclined to admit, perhaps to desire, the intervention of the superhuman; but, for all that, there are few, even among the most mystic, who are not convinced that our moral misfortunes are, in their essence, determined by our mind and our character; and, similarly, that our physical misfortunes are due in part to the workings of certain forces which often are misunderstood, and in part to the generally ill-defined relation of cause to effect: nor is it unreasonable to hope that light may be thrown on these problems as we penetrate further into the secrets of nature. We have here a certitude upon which our whole life depends; a certitude which is shaken only when we consider our own misfortunes, for then we shrink from analysing or admitting the faults we ourselves have committed. There is a hopefulness in man which renders him unwilling to grant that the cause of his misfortune may be as transparent as that of the wave which dies away in the sand or is hurled on the cliff, of the insect whose little wings gleam for an instant in the light of the sun till the passing bird absorbs its existence.

21

Let me suppose that a neighbour of mine, whom I know very intimately, whose regular habits and inoffensive manners have won my esteem, should successively lose his wife in a railway accident, one son at sea, another in a fire, the third and last by disease. I should, of course, be painfully shocked and grieved; but still it would not occur to me to attribute this series of disasters to a divine vengeance or an invisible justice, to a strange, ill-starred predestination, or an active, persistent, inevitable fatality. My thoughts would fly to the myriad unfortunate hazards of life; I should be appalled at the frightful coincidence of calamity; but in me there would be no suggestion of a superhuman will that had hurled the train over the precipice, steered the ship on to rocks, or kindled the flames; I should hold it incredible that such monstrous efforts could have been put forth with the sole object of inflicting punishment and despair upon a poor wretch, because of some error he might have committed—one of those grave human errors which yet are so petty in face of the universe; an error which perhaps had not issued from either his heart or his brain, and had stirred not one blade of grass on the earth's whole surface.

22

But he, this neighbour of mine, on whom these terrible blows have successively fallen, like so many lightning-flashes on a black night of storm—will he think as I do; will these catastrophes seem natural to him, and ordinary, and susceptible of explanation? Will not the words destiny, fortune, hazard, ill-luck, fatality, star—the word Providence, perhaps—assume in his mind a significance they never have assumed before? Will not the light beneath which he questions his consciousness be a different light from my own, will he not feel round his life an influence, a power, a kind of evil intention, that are imperceptible to me? And who is right, he or I? Which of us two sees more clearly, and further? Do truths that in calmer times lie hidden float to the surface in hours of trouble; and which is the moment we should choose to establish the meaning of life?

The "interpreter of life," as a rule, selects the troubled hours. He places himself, and us, in the soul-state of his victims. He shows their misfortunes to us in perspective; and so sharply, concretely, that we have for the moment the illusion of a personal disaster. And, indeed, it is more or less impossible for him to depict them as they would occur in real life. If we had spent long years with the hero of the drama which has stirred us so painfully, had he been our brother, our father, our friend, we should have probably noted, recognised, counted one by one as they passed, all the causes of his misfortune, which then would not only appear less extraordinary to us, but perfectly natural even, and humanly almost inevitable. But to the "interpreter of life" is given neither power nor occasion to acquaint us with each veritable cause. For these causes, as a rule, are infinitely slow in their movement, and countless in number, and slight, and of small apparent significance. He is therefore led to adopt a general cause, one sufficiently vast to embrace the whole drama, in place of the real and human causes which he is unable to show us, unable, too, himself to examine and study. And where shall a general cause of sufficient vastness be found, if not in the two or three words we breathe to ourselves when silence oppresses us: words like fatality, divinity, Providence, or obscure and nameless justice?

23

The question we have to consider is how far this procedure can be beneficial, or even legitimate; as also whether it be the mission of the poet to present, and insist on, the distress and confusion of our least lucid hours, or to add to the clear-sightedness of the moments when we conceive ourselves to enjoy the fullest possession of our force and our reason. In our own misfortunes there is something of good, and something of good must therefore be found in the illusion of personal misfortune. We are made to look into ourselves; our errors, our weaknesses, are more clearly revealed; it is shown to us where we have strayed. There falls a light on our consciousness a thousand times more searching, more active, than could spring from many arduous years of meditation and study. We are forced to emerge from ourselves, and to let our eyes rest on those round about us; we are rendered more keenly alive to the sorrows of others. There are some who will tell us that misfortune does even more—that it urges our glance on high, and compels us to bow to a power superior to our own, to an unseen justice, to an impenetrable, infinite mystery. Can this indeed be the best of all possible issues? Ah, yes, it was well, from the standpoint of religious morality, that misfortune should teach us to lift up our eyes and look on an eternal, unchanging, undeniable God, sovereignly beautiful, sovereignly just, and sovereignly good. It was well that the poet who found in his God an unquestionable ideal should incessantly hold before us this unique, this definitive ideal. But to-day, if we look away from the truth, from the ordinary experience of life, on what shall our eager glance rest? If we discard the more or less compensatory laws of conscience and inward happiness, what shall we say when triumphant injustice confronts us, or successful, unpunished crime? How shall we account for the death of a child, the miserable end of an innocent man, or the disaster hurled by cruel fate on some unfortunate creature, if we seek explanations loftier, more definite, more comprehensive and decisive than those that are found satisfactory in everyday life for the reason that they are the only ones that accord with a certain number of realities? Is it right that the poet, in his eager desire to contrive a solemn atmosphere for his drama, should arouse from their slumber sentiments, errors, prejudices and fears, which we would attack and rebuke were we to discover them in the hearts of our friends or our children? Man has at last, through his study of the habits of spirit and brain, of the laws of existence, the caprices of fate and the maternal indifference of nature— man has at last, and laboriously, acquired some few certitudes, that are worthy of all respect; and is the poet entitled to seize on the moment of anguish in order to oust all these certitudes, and set up in their place a fatality to which every action of ours gives the lie; or powers before which we would refuse to kneel did the blow fall on us that has prostrated his hero; or a mystic justice that, for all it may sweep away the need for many an embarrassing explanation, bears yet not the slightest kinship to the active and personal justice we all of us recognise in our own personal life?

24

And yet this is what the "interpreter of life" will more or less deliberately do from the moment he seeks to invest his work with a lofty spirit, with a deep and religious beauty, with the sense of the infinite. Even though this work of his may be of the sincerest, though it express as nearly as may be his own most intimate truth, he believes that this truth is enhanced, and established more firmly, by being surrounded with phantoms of a forgotten past. Might not the symbols he needs, the hypotheses, images, the touchstone for all that cannot be explained, be less frequently sought in that which he knows is not true, and more often in that which will one day be a truth? Does the unearthing of bygone terrors, or the borrowing of light from a Hell that has ceased to be, make death more sublime? Does dependence on a supreme but imaginary will ennoble our destiny? Does justice—that vast network woven by human action and reaction over the unchanging wisdom of nature's moral and physical forces—does justice become more majestic through being lodged in the hands of a unique judge, whom the very spirit of the drama dethrones and destroys?

25

Let us ask ourselves whether the hour may not have come for the earnest revision of the symbols, the images, sentiments, beauty, wherewith we still seek to glorify in us the spectacle of the world.

This beauty, these feelings and sentiments, to-day

unquestionably bear only the most distant relation to the phenomena, thoughts, nay even the dreams, of our actual existence; and if they are suffered still to abide with us, it is rather as tender and innocent memories of a past that was more credulous, and nearer to the childhood of man. Were it not well, then, that those whose mission it is to make more evident to us the beauty and harmony of the world we live in, should march ever onwards, and let their steps tend to the actual truth of this world? Their conception of the universe need not be stripped of a single one of the ornaments wherewith they embellish it; but why seek these ornaments so often among mere recollections, however smiling or terrible, and so seldom from among the essential thoughts which have helped these men to build, and effectively organise, their spiritual and sentient life?

It can never be right to dwell in the midst of false images, even though these are known to be false. The time will come when the illusory image will usurp the place of the just idea it has seemed to represent. We shall not reduce the part of the infinite and the mysterious by employing other images, by framing other and juster conceptions. Do what we may, this part can never be lessened. It will always be found deep down in the heart of men, at the root of each problem, pervading the universe. And for all that the substance, the place of these mysteries, may seem to have changed, their extent and power remain for ever the same. Has not—to take but one instance—has not the phenomenon of the existence, everywhere among us, of a kind of supreme and wholly spiritual justice, unarmed, unadorned, unequipped, moving slowly but never swerving, stable and changeless in a world where injustice would seem to reign—has this phenomenon not cause and effect as deep, as exhaustless—is it not as astounding, as admirable—as the wisdom of an eternal and omnipresent Judge? Should this Judge be held more convincing for that He is less conceivable? Are fewer

Maurice Maeterlinck

sources of beauty, or occasions for genius to exercise insight and power, to be found in what can be explained than in what is, *a priori*, inexplicable? Does not, for instance, a victorious but unjust war (such as those of the Romans, of England to-day, the conquests of Spain in America, and so many others) in the end always demoralise the victor and thrust upon him errors, habits, and faults whereby he is made to pay dearly for his triumph; and is not the minute, the relentless labour of this psychological justice as absorbing, as vast, as the intervention of a superhuman justice? And may not the same be said of the justice that lives in each one of us, that causes the space left for peace, inner happiness, love, to expand or contract in our mind and our heart in the degree of our striving towards that which is just or is unjust?

26

And to turn to one mystery more, the most awful of all, that of death—would any one pretend that our perception of justice, of goodness and beauty, or our intellectual, sentient power, our eagerness for all that draws near to the infinite, all-powerful, eternal, has dwindled since death ceased to be held the immense and exclusive anguish of life? Does not each new generation find the burden lighter to bear as the forms of death grow less violent and its posthumous terrors fade? It is the illness that goes before, the physical pain, of which we are to-day most afraid. But death is no longer the hour of the wrathful, inscrutable judge; no longer the one and the terrible goal, the gulf of misery and eternal punishment. It is slowly becoming—indeed, in some cases, it has already become—the wished-for repose of a life that draws to its end. Its weight no longer oppresses each one of our actions; and, above all—for this is the most striking change—it has ceased to intrude itself into our morality. And is this morality of ours less lofty, less pure, less profound, because of the disinterestedness it has thus acquired? Has the loss of an overwhelming dread robbed mankind of a single precious, indispensable feeling? And must not life itself find gain in the importance wrested from death? Surely: for the neutral forces we hold in reserve within us are waiting and ready; and every discouragement, sorrow, or fear that departs has its place quickly filled by a certitude, admiration, or hope.

27

The poet is inclined to personify fatality and justice, and give outward form to forces really within us, for the reason that to show them at work in ourselves is a matter of exceeding difficulty; and further, that the unknown and the infinite, to the extent that they *are* unknown and infinite—*i.e.* lacking personality, intelligence, and morality—are powerless to move us. And here it is curious to note that we are in no degree affected by material mystery, however dangerous or obscure, or by psychological justice, however involved its results. It is not the incomprehensible in nature that masters and crushes us, but the thought that nature may possibly be governed by a conscious, superior, reasoning will; one that, although superhuman, has yet some kinship with the will of man. What we dread, in a word, is the presence of a God; and speak as we may of fatality, justice, or mystery, it is always God whom we fear: a being, that is, like ourselves, though almighty, eternal, invisible, and infinite. A moral force that was not conceived in the image of man would most likely inspire no fear. It is not the unknown in nature that fills us with dread; it is not the mystery of the world we live in. It is the mystery of another world from which we recoil; it is the moral and not the material enigma. There is nothing, for instance, more obscure than the combination of causes which produce the earthquake, that most terrible of all catastrophes. But the earthquake, though it alarm our body,

Maurice Maeterlinck

will bring no fear to our mind unless we regard it as an act of justice, of mysterious vengeance, of supernatural punishment. And so it is, too, with the thunderstorm, with illness, with death, with the myriad phenomena and accidents of life. It would seem as though the true alarm of our soul, the great fear which stirs other instincts within us than that of mere self-preservation, is only called forth by the thought of a more or less determinate God, of a mysterious consciousness, a permanent, invisible justice, or a vigilant, eternal Providence. But does the "interpreter of life," who succeeds in arousing this fear, bring us nearer to truth; and is it his mission to convey to us sorrow, and trouble, and painful emotion, or peace, satisfaction, tranquillity, and light?

28

It is not easy, I know, to free oneself wholly from traditional interpretation, for it often succeeds in reasserting its sway upon us at the very moment we strain every nerve to escape from our bondage. So has it happened with Ibsen, who, in his search for a new and almost scientific form of fatality, erected the veiled, majestic, tyrannical figure of heredity in the centre of the very best of his dramas. But it is not the scientific mystery of heredity which awakens within us those human fears that lie so much deeper than the mere animal fear; for heredity alone could no more achieve this result than could the scientific mystery of a dreaded disease, a stellar or marine phenomenon. No, the fear that differs so essentially from the one called forth by an imminent natural danger, is aroused within us by the obscure idea of justice which heredity assumes in the drama; by the daring pronouncement that the sins of the fathers are almost invariably visited on the children; by the suggestion that a sovereign Judge, a goddess of the species, is for ever watching our actions, inscribing them on her tablets of bronze, and balancing in her eternal hands rewards long deferred and never-ending punishment. In a word, even while we deny it, it is the face of God that reappears; and from beneath the flagstone one had believed to be sealed for ever comes once again the murmur of the very ancient flame of Hell.

29

This new form of fatality, or fatal justice, is less defensible, and less acceptable too, than the ancient and elementary power, which, being general and undefined, and offering no too strict explanation of its actions, lent itself to a far greater number of situations. In the special case selected by Ibsen, it is not impossible that some kind of accidental justice may be found, as it is not impossible that the arrow a blind man shoots into a crowd may chance to strike a parricide. But to found a law upon this accidental justice is a fresh perversion of mystery, for elements are thereby introduced into human morality which have no right to be there; elements which we would welcome, which would be of value, if they stood for definite truths; but seeing that they are as alien to truth as to actual life, they should be ruthlessly swept aside. I have shown elsewhere that our experience fails to detect the most minute trace of justice in the phenomena of heredity; or, in other words, that it fails to discover the slightest moral connection between the cause: the fault of the father, and the effect: the punishment or reward of the child.

The poet has the right to fashion hypotheses, and to forge his way ahead of reality. But it will often happen that when he imagines himself to be far in advance, he will truly have done no more than turn in a circle; that where he believes that he has discovered new truth, he has merely strayed on to the track of a buried illusion. In the case I have named, for the poet to have taught us more than experience teaches, he should have ventured still further, perhaps, in the negation of justice. But whatever our opinion may be on this point, it at least is clear that the poet who desires his hypotheses to be legitimate, and of service, must take heed that they be not too manifestly contrary to the experience of everyday life; for in that case they become useless and dangerous—scarcely honourable even, if the error be deliberately made.

30

And now, what are we to conclude from all this? Many things, if one will, but this above all: that it behoves the "interpreter of life," no less than those who are living that life, to exercise greatest care in their manner of handling and admitting mystery, and to discard the belief that whatever is noblest and best in life or in drama must of necessity rest in the part that admits of no explanation. There are many most beautiful, most human, most admirable works which are almost entirely free from this "disquiet of universal mystery." We derive no greatness, sublimity, or depth from unceasingly fixing our thoughts on the infinite and the unknown. Such meditation becomes truly helpful only when it is the unexpected reward of the mind that has loyally, unreservedly, given itself to the study of the finite and the knowable; and to such a mind it will soon be revealed how strangely different is the mystery which precedes what one does not know from the mystery that follows closely on what one has learned. The first would seem to contain many sorrows, but that is only because the sorrows are grouped there too closely, and have their home upon two of three peaks that stand too nearly together. In the second is far less sadness, for its area is vast; and when the horizon is wide, there exists no sorrow so great but it takes the form of a hope.

31

Yes, human life, viewed as a whole, may appear somewhat sorrowful; and it is easier, in a manner pleasanter even, to speak of its sorrows and let the mind dwell on them, than to go in search of, and bring into prominence, the consolations life has to offer. Sorrows abound—infallible, evident sorrows; consolations, or rather the reasons wherefore we accept with some gladness the duty of life, are rare and uncertain, and hard of detection. Sorrows seem noble, and lofty, and fraught with deep mystery; with mystery that almost is personal, that we feel to be near to us. Consolations appear egotistical, squalid, at times almost base. But for all that, and whatever their ephemeral likeness may be, we have only to draw closer to them to find that they too have their mystery; and if this seem less visible and less comprehensible, it is only because it lies deeper and is far more mysterious. The desire to live, the acceptance of life as it is, may perhaps be mere vulgar expressions; but yet they are probably in unconscious harmony with laws that are vaster, more conformable with the spirit of the universe, and therefore more sacred, than is the desire to escape the sorrows of life, or the lofty but disenchanted wisdom that for ever dwells on those sorrows.

32

Our impulse is always to depict life as more sorrowful than truly it is; and this is a serious error, to be excused only by the doubts that at present hang over us. No satisfying explanation has so far been found. The destiny of man is as subject to unknown forces to-day as it was in the days of old; and though it be true that some of these forces have vanished, others have arisen in their stead. The number of those that are really all-powerful has in no way diminished.

Many attempts have been made, and in countless fashions, to explain the action of these forces and account for their intervention; and one might almost believe that the poets, aware of the futility of these explanations in face of a reality which, all things notwithstanding, is ever revealing more and more of itself, have fallen back on fatality as in some measure representing the inexplicable, or at least the sadness of the inexplicable. This is all that we find in Ibsen, the Russian novels, the highest class of modern fiction, Flaubert, &c. (see "War and Peace," for instance, *L'Education Sentimentale*, and many others).

It is true that the fatality shown is no longer the goddess of old, or rather (at least to the bulk of mankind) the clearly determinate God, inflexible, implacable, arbitrary, blind, although constantly watchful; the fatality of to-day is vaster, more formless, more vague, less human or actively personal, more indifferent and more universal. In a word, it is now no more than a provisional appellation bestowed, until better be found, on the general and inexplicable misery of man. In this sense we may accept it, perhaps, though we do no more than give a new name to the unchanging enigma, and throw no light on the darkness. But we have no right to exaggerate its importance or the part that it plays; no right to believe that we are truly surveying mankind and events from a point of some loftiness, beneath a definitive light, or that there is nothing to seek beyond, because at times we become deeply conscious of the obscure and invincible force that lies at the end of every existence. Doubtless, from one point of view, unhappiness must always remain the portion of man, and the fatal abyss be ever open before him, vowed as he is to death, to the fickleness of matter, to old age and disease. If we fix our eyes only upon the end of a life, the happiest and most triumphant existence must of necessity contain its elements of misery and fatality. But let us not make a wrong use of these words; above all, let us not, through listlessness or undue inclination to mystic sorrow, be induced to lessen the part of what could be explained if we would only give more eager attention to the ideas, the passions and feelings of the life of man and the nature of things. Let us always remember that we are steeped in the unknown; for this thought is the most fruitful of all, the most sustaining and salutary. But the neutrality of the unknown does not warrant our attributing to it a force, or designs, or hostility, which it cannot be proved to possess. At Erfurt, in his famous interview with Goethe, Napoleon is said to have spoken disparagingly of the dramas in which fatality plays a great part—the plays that we, in our "passion for calamity," are apt to consider the finest. "They belong," he remarked, "to an epoch of darkness; but how can fatality touch us to-day? Policy—*that* is fatality!" Napoleon's dictum is not very profound: policy is only the merest fragment of fatality; and his destiny very soon made it manifest to him that the desire to contain fatality within the narrow bounds of policy was no more than a vain endeavour to imprison in a fragile vase the mightiest of the spiritual rivers that bathe our globe. And yet, incomplete as this thought of Napoleon's may have been, it still throws some light on a tributary of the great river. It was a little thing, perhaps, but on these uncertain shores it is the difference between a little thing and nothing that kindles the energy of man and confirms his destiny. By this ray of light, such as it was, he long was enabled to dominate all that portion of the unknown which he declined to term fatality. To us who come after him, the portion of the unknown that he controlled may well seem insufficient, if surveyed from an eminence, and yet it was truly one of the vastest that the eye of man has ever embraced. Through its means every action of his was accomplished, for evil or good. This is not the place to judge him, or even to wonder whether the happiness of a century might not have been better served had he allowed events to guide him; what we are considering here is the docility of the unknown. For us, with our humbler destinies, the problem

Maurice Maeterlinck

still is the same, and the principle too; the principle being that of Goethe: "to stand on the outermost limit of the conceivable; but never to overstep this line, for beyond it begins at once the land of chimeras, the phantoms and mists of which are fraught with danger to the mind." It is only when the intervention of the mysterious, invisible, or irresistible becomes strikingly real, actually perceptible, intelligent, and moral, that we are entitled to yield or lay down our arms, meekly accepting the inactive silence they bring; but their intervention, within these limits, is rarer than one imagines. Let us recognise that mystery of this kind exists; but, until it reveal itself, we have not the right to halt, or relax our efforts; not the right to cast down our eyes in submission, or resign ourselves to silence.

III

THE KINGDOM OF MATTER

1

In a preceding essay we were compelled to admit that, eager as man might be to discover in the universe a sanction for his virtues, neither heaven nor earth displayed the least interest in human morality; and that all things would combine to persuade the upright among us that they merely are dupes, were it not for the fact that they have in themselves an approval words cannot describe, and a reward so intangible that we should in vain endeavour to portray its least evanescent delights. Is that all, some may ask, is that all we may hope in return for this mighty effort of ours, for our constant denial and pain, for our sacrifice of instincts, of pleasures, that seemed so legitimate, necessary even, and would certainly have added to our happiness had there not been within us the desire for Justice—a desire arising we know not whence, belonging, perhaps, to our nature, and yet in apparent conflict with the vaster nature whereof we all form part? Yes, it is open to you, if you choose, to regard as a very poor thing this unsubstantial justice: since its only reward is a vague satisfaction, and that this satisfaction even grows hateful, and destroys itself, the moment its presence becomes too perceptibly felt. Bear in mind, however, that all

Maurice Maeterlinck

things that happen in our moral being must be equally lightly held, if regarded from the point of view whence you deliver this judgment. Love is a paltry affair, the moment of possession once over that alone is real and ensures the perpetuity of the race; and yet we find that as man grows more civilised, the act of possession assumes ever less value in his eyes if there go not with it, if there do not precede, accompany, and follow it, the insignificant emotion built up of our thoughts and our feelings, of our sweetest and tenderest hours and years. Beauty, too, is a trivial matter: a beautiful spectacle, a beautiful face, or body, or gesture: a melodious voice, or noble statue—sunrise at sea, flowers in a garden, stars shining over the forest, the river by moonlight—or a lofty thought, an exquisite poem, an heroic sacrifice hidden in a profound and pitiful soul. We may admire these things for an instant; they may bring us a sense of completeness no other joy can convey; but at the same time there will steal over us a tinge of strange sorrow, unrest; nor will they give happiness to us, as men use the word, should other events have contrived to make us unhappy. They produce nothing the eye can measure, or weigh; nothing that others can see, or will envy; and yet, were a magician suddenly to appear, capable of depriving one of us of this sense of beauty that may chance to be in him, possessed of the power of extinguishing it for ever, with no trace remaining, no hope that it ever will spring into being again—would we not rather lose riches, tranquillity, health even, and many years of our life, than this strange faculty which none can espy, and we ourselves can scarcely define? Not less intangible, not less elusive, is the sweetness of tender friendship, of a dear recollection we cling to and reverence; and countless other thoughts and feelings, that traverse no mountain, dispel no cloud, that do not even dislodge a grain of sand by the roadside. But these are the things that build up what is best and happiest in us; they are we, ourselves; they are precisely what those who have them not should envy in those who have. The more we emerge from the animal, and approach what seems the surest ideal of our race, the more evident does it become that these things, trifling as they well may appear by the side of nature's stupendous laws, do yet constitute our sole inheritance; and that, happen what may to the end of time, they are the hearth, the centre of light, to which mankind will draw ever more and more closely.

2

We live in a century that loves the material, but, while loving it, conquers it, masters it, and with more passion than any preceding period has shown; in a century that would seem consumed with desire to comprehend matter, to penetrate, enslave it, possess it once and for all to repletion, satiety—with the wish, it may be, to ransack its every resource, lay bare its last secret, thereby freeing the future from the restless search for a happiness there seemed reason once to believe that matter contained. So, in like manner, is it necessary first to have known the love of the flesh before the veritable love can reveal its deep and unchanging purity. A serious reaction will probably arise, some day, against this passion for material enjoyment; but man will never be able to cast himself wholly free. Nor would the attempt be wise. We are, after all, only fragments of animate matter, and it could not be well to lose sight of the starting-point of our race. And yet, is it right that this starting-point should enclose in its narrow circumference all our wishes, all our happiness, the totality of our desires? In our passage through life we meet scarcely any who do not persist, with a kind of unreasoning obstinacy, in throning the material within them, and there maintaining it supreme. Gather together a number of men and women, all of them free from life's more depressing cares—an assembly of the elect, if you will—and pronounce before them the words "beatitude, happiness, joy, felicity, ideal." Imagine that an angel, at that very instant, were to seize and retain, in a magic mirror or miraculous basket, the images these words would evoke in the souls that should hear them. What would you see in the basket or mirror? The embrace of beautiful bodies; gold, precious stones, a palace, an ample park; the philtre of youth, strange jewels and gauds representing vanity's dreams; and, let us admit it, prominent far above all would be sumptuous repasts, noble wines, glittering tables, splendid apartments. Is humanity still too near its beginning to conceive other things? Has the hour not arrived when we might have reasonably hoped the mirror to reflect a powerful, disinterested intellect, a conscience at rest: a just and loving heart, a perception, a vision capable of detecting, absorbing beauty wherever it be—the beauty of evening, of cities, of forests and seas, no less than of face, of a word or a smile, of an action or movement of soul? The foreground of the magical mirror at present reflects beautiful women, undraped; when shall we see, in their stead, the deep, great love of two beings to whom the knowledge has come that it is only when their thoughts and their feelings, and all that is more mysterious still than thoughts and feelings, have blended, and day by day become more essentially one, that the joys of the flesh are freed from the after disquiet, and leave no bitterness behind? When shall we find, instead of the morbid, unnatural excitement produced by too copious, oppressive repasts, by stimulants that are the insidious agents of the very enemy we seek to destroy—when shall we find, in their place, the contained and deliberate gladness of a spirit that is for ever exalted because it for ever is seeking to understand, and to love? . . . These things have long been known, and their repetition may well seem of little avail. And yet, we need but to have been twice or thrice in the company of those who stand for what is best in mankind, most intellectually, sentiently human, to realise how uncertain and groping their search is still for the happier hours of life; to marvel at the resemblance the unconscious happiness they look for bears to the happiness craved by the man who has no spiritual existence; to note how opaque, to their eyes, is the cloud which separates all that pertains to the being who rises from all that is his who descends. Some will say that the hour is not yet when man can thus make clear division between the part of the spirit and that of the flesh. But when shall that hour be looked for if those for whom it should long since have sounded still suffer the obscurest prejudice of the mass to guide them when they set forth in search of their happiness? When they achieve glory and riches, when love comes to meet them, they will be free, it may be, from a few of the coarser satisfactions of vanity, a few of the grosser excesses; but beyond this they strive not at all to secure a happiness that shall be more spiritual, more purely human. The advantage they have does not teach them to widen the circle of material exaction, to discard what is less justifiable. In their attitude towards the pleasures of life they submit to the same spiritual deprivation as, let us say, some cultured man who may have wandered into a theatre where the play being performed is not one of the five or six masterpieces of universal literature. He is fully aware that his neighbours' applause and delight are called forth, in the main, by more or less obnoxious prejudices on the subject of honour, glory, religion, patriotism, sacrifice, liberty, or love —or perhaps by some feeble, dreary poetical effusion. None the less, he will find himself affected by the general enthusiasm; and it will be necessary for him, almost at every instant, to pull himself violently together, to make startled appeal to every conviction within him, in order to convince himself that these partisans of hoary errors are wrong, notwithstanding their number, and that he, with his isolated reason, alone is right.

3

Indeed, when we consider the relation of man to matter, it is surprising to find how little light has yet been thrown upon it, how little has been definitely fixed. Elementary, imperious, as this relation undoubtedly is, humanity has always been wavering, uncertain, passing from the most dangerous confidence to the most systematic distrust, from adoration to horror, from asceticism and complete renouncement to their corresponding extremes. The days are past when an irrational, useless abstinence was preached, and put into practice—an abstinence often fully as harmful as habitual excess. We are entitled to all that helps to maintain, or advance, the development of the body; this is our right, but it has its limits; and these limits it would be well to define with the utmost exactness, for whatever may trespass beyond must infallibly weaken the growth of that other side of ourselves, the flower that the leaves round about it will either stifle or nourish. And humanity, that so long has been watching this flower, studying it so intently, noting its subtlest, most fleeting perfumes and shades, is most often content to abandon to the caprice of the temperament, be this evil or good, to the passing moment, or to chance, the government of the unconscious forces that will, like the leaves, be discreetly active, sustaining, life-giving, or profoundly selfish, destructive, and fatal. Hitherto, perhaps, this may have been done with impunity; for the ideal of mankind (which at the start was concerned with the body alone) wavered long between matter and spirit. To-day, however, it clings, with ever profounder conviction, to the human intelligence. We no longer strive to compete with the lion, the panther, the great anthropoid ape, in force or agility; in beauty with the flower or the shine of the stars on the sea. The utilisation by our intellect of every unconscious force, the gradual subjugation of matter and the search for its secret—these at present appear the most evident aim of our race, and its most probable mission. In the days of doubt there was no satisfaction, or even excess, but was excusable, and moral, so long as it wrought no irreparable loss of strength or actual organic harm. But now that the mission of the race is becoming more clearly defined, the duty is on us to leave on one side whatever is not directly helpful to the spiritual part of our being. Sterile pleasures of the body must be gradually sacrificed; indeed, in a word, all that is not in absolute harmony with a larger, more durable energy of thought; all the little "harmless" delights which, however inoffensive comparatively, keep alive by example and habit the prejudice in favour of inferior enjoyment, and usurp the place that belongs to the satisfactions of the intellect. These last differ from those of the body, whose development some may assist and others retard. Into the elysian fields of thought enters no satisfaction but brings with it youth, and strength, and ardour; nor is there a thing in this world on which the mind thrives more readily than the ecstasy, nay, the debauch, of eagerness, comprehension, and wonder.

4

The time must come, sooner or later, when our morality will have to conform to the probable mission of the race; when the arbitrary, often ridiculous restrictions whereof it is at present composed will be compelled to make way for the inevitable logical restrictions this mission exacts. For the individual, as for the race, there can be but one code of morals—the subordination of the ways of life to the demands of the general mission that appears entrusted to man. The axis will shift, therefore, of many sins, many great offences; until at last for all the crimes against the body there shall be substituted the veritable crimes against human destiny; in other words, whatever may tend to impair the authority, integrity, leisure, liberty, or power of the intellect.

Maurice Maeterlinck

But by this we are far from suggesting that the body should be regarded as the irreconcilable enemy which the Christian theory holds it. Far from that, we should strive, first of all, to endow it with all possible vigour and beauty. But it is like a capricious child: exacting, improvident, selfish; and the stronger it grows the more dangerous does it become. It knows no cult but that of the passing moment. In imagination, desires, it halts at the trivial thought, the primitive, fleeting, foolish delight of the little dog or the negro. The satisfactions procured by the intellect—the comfort, security, leisure, the gladness—it regards as no more than its due, and enjoys in fullest complacency. Left to itself, it would enjoy these so stupidly, savagely, that it would very soon stifle the intellect from which it derived these favours. Hence there is need for certain restrictions, renouncements, which all men must observe; not only those who have reason to hope, and believe, that they are effectively striving to solve the enigma, to bring about the fulfilment of human destiny and the triumph of mind over insensible matter, but also the crowds in the ranks of the massive, unconscious rearguard, who placidly watch the phosphorescent evolutions of mind as its light gleams on the world's elementary darkness. For humanity is a unique and unanimous entity. When the thought of the mass—that thought which scarcely is thought —travels downwards, its influence is felt by philosopher and poet, astronomer and chemist; it has its pronounced effect on their character, morals, ideals, their sense of duty, habits of labour, intellectual vigour. If the myriad, uniform, petty ideas in the valley fall short of a certain elevation, no great idea shall spring to life on the mountain-peak. Down there the thought may have little strength, but there are countless numbers who think it; and the influence this thought acquires may be almost termed atmospheric. And they up above on the mountain, the precipice, the edge of the glacier, will be helped by this influence, or harmed, in the degree of its brightness or gloom, of its reaching them, buoyed up with generous feeling, or heavily charged with brutal habit and coarse desire. The heroic action of a people (as, for instance, the French Revolution, the Reformation, all wars of independence and liberation) will fertilise and purify this people for more centuries than one. But far less will satisfy those who toil at the fulfilment of destiny. Let but the habits of the men round about them become a little more noble, their desires a little more disinterested; let but their passions and eagerness, their pleasures and love, be illumined by one ray of brightness, of grace, of spiritual fervour; and those up above will feel the support, and draw their breath freely, no longer compelled to struggle with the instinctive part of themselves; and the power that is in them will obey the more readily, and mould itself to their hand. The peasant who, instead of carousing at the beershop, spends a peaceful Sunday at home, with a book, beneath the trees of his orchard; the humble citizen whom the emotions or din of the racecourse cannot tempt from some worthy enjoyment, from the pleasure of a reposeful afternoon; the workman who no longer makes the streets hideous with obscene or ridiculous song, but wanders forth into the country, or, from the ramparts, watches the sunset—all these bring their meed of help: their great assistance, unconscious though it be, and anonymous, to the triumph of the vast human flame.

5

But how much there is to be done, and learned, before this great flame can arise in serene, secure brightness! We have said that man, in his relation to matter, is still in the experimental, groping stage of his earliest days. He lacks even definite knowledge as to the kind of food best adapted for him, or the quantity of nourishment he requires; he is still uncertain as to whether he be carnivorous or frugivorous. His intellect misleads his instinct. It was only yesterday that he learned that he had probably erred hitherto in the choice of his nourishment; that he must reduce by two-thirds the quantity of nitrogen he absorbs, and largely increase the volume of hydrocarbons; that a little fruit, or milk, a few vegetables, farinaceous substances—now the mere accessory of the too plentiful repasts which he works so hard to provide, which are his chief object in life, the goal of his efforts, of his strenuous, incessant labour—are amply sufficient to maintain the ardour of the finest and mightiest life. It is not my purpose here to discuss the question of vegetarianism, or to meet the objections that may be urged against it; though it must be admitted that of these objections not one can withstand a loyal and scrupulous inquiry. I, for my part, can affirm that those whom I have known to submit themselves to this regimen have found its result to be improved or restored health, marked addition of strength, and the acquisition by the mind of a clearness, brightness, well-being, such as might follow the release from some secular, loathsome, detestable dungeon. But we must not conclude these pages with an essay on alimentation, reasonable as such a proceeding might be. For in truth all our justice, morality, all our thoughts and feelings, derive from three or four primordial necessities, whereof the principal one is food. The least modification of one of these necessities would entail a marked change in our moral existence. Were the belief one day to become general that man could dispense with animal food, there would ensue not only a great economic revolution—for a bullock, to produce one pound of meat, consumes more than a hundred of provender —but a moral improvement as well, not less important and certainly more sincere and more lasting than might follow a second appearance on the earth of the Envoy of the Father, come to remedy the errors and omissions of his former pilgrimage. For we find that the man who abandons the regimen of meat abandons alcohol also; and to do this is to renounce most of the coarser and more degraded pleasures of life. And it is in the passionate craving for these pleasures, in their glamour, and the prejudice they create, that the most formidable obstacle is found to the harmonious development of the race. Detachment therefrom creates noble leisure, a new order of desires, a wish for enjoyment that must of necessity be loftier than the gross satisfactions which have their origin in alcohol. But are days such as these in store for us—these happier, purer hours? The crime of alcohol is not alone that it destroys its faithful and poisons one half of the race, but also that it exercises a profound, though indirect, influence upon those who recoil from it in dread. The idea of pleasure which it maintains in the crowd forces its way, by means of the crowd's irresistible action, into the life even of the elect, and lessens, perverts, all that concerns man's peace and repose, his expansiveness, gladness and joy; retarding, too, it may safely be said, the birth of the truer, profounder ideal of happiness: one that shall be simpler, more peaceful and grave, more spiritual and human. This ideal is evidently still very imaginary, and may seem of but little importance; and infinite time must elapse, as in all other cases, before the certitude of those who are convinced that the race so far has erred in the choice of its aliment (assuming the truth of this statement to be borne out by experience) shall reach the confused masses, and bring them enlightenment and comfort. But may this not be the expedient Nature holds in reserve for the time when the struggle for life shall have become too hopelessly unbearable—the struggle for life that to-day means the fight for meat and for alcohol, double source of injustice and waste whence all the others are fed, double symbol of a happiness and necessity whereof neither is human?

6

Whither is humanity tending? This anxiety of man to know

the aim and the end is essentially human; it is a kind of infirmity or provincialism of the mind, and has nothing in common with universal reality. Have things an aim? Why should they have; and what aim or end can there be, in an infinite organism?

But even though our mission be only to fill for an instant a diminutive space that could as well be filled by the violet or grasshopper, without loss to the universe of economy or grandeur, without the destinies of this world being shortened or lengthened thereby by one hour; even though this march of ours count for nothing, though we move but for the sake of motion, tending no-whither, this futile progress may nevertheless still claim to absorb all our attention and interest; and this is entirely reasonable, it is the loftiest course we can pursue. If it lay in the power of an ant to study the laws of the stars; and if, intent on this study, though fully aware that these laws are immutable, never to be modified, it declined to concern itself further with the affairs or the future of the anthill—should we, who stand to the insect as the great gods are supposed to stand to ourselves, who judge it and dominate it, as we believe ourselves to be dominated and judged; should we approve this ant, or, for all its universality, regard it as either good or moral?

Reason, at its apogee, becomes sterile; and inertia would be its sole teaching did it not, after recognising the pettiness, the nothingness, of our passions and hopes, of our being, and lastly, of reason itself, retrace its footsteps back to the point whence it shall be able once more to take eager interest in all these poor trivialities, in this same nothingness, as holding them the only things in the world for which its assistance has value.

We know not whither we go, but may still rejoice in the journey; and this will become the lighter, the happier, for our endeavour to picture to ourselves the next place of halt. Where will this be? The mountain-pass lies ahead, and threatens; but the roads already are widening and becoming less rugged; the trees spread their branches, crowned with fresh blossom; silent waters are flowing before us, reposeful and peaceful. Tokens all these, it may be, of our nearing the vastest valley mankind yet has seen from the height of the tortuous paths it has ever been climbing! Shall we call it the "First Valley of Leisure"? Distrust as we may the surprises the future may have in store, be the troubles and cares that await us never so burdensome, there still seems some ground for believing that the bulk of mankind will know days when, thanks, it may be, to machinery, agricultural chemistry, medicine perhaps, or I know not what dawning science, labour will become less incessant, exhausting, less material, tyrannical, pitiless. What use will humanity make of this leisure? On its employment may be said to depend the whole destiny of man. Were it not well that his counsellors now should begin to teach him to use such leisure he has in a nobler and worthier fashion? It is the way in which hours of freedom are spent that determines, as much as war or as labour, the moral worth of a nation. It raises or lowers, it replenishes or exhausts. At present we find, in these great cities of ours, that three days' idleness will fill the hospitals with victims whom weeks or months of toil had left unscathed.

7

Thus we return to the happiness which should be, and perhaps in course of time will be, the real human happiness. Had we taken part in the creation of the world, we should probably have bestowed more special, distinctive force on all that is best in man, most immaterial, most essentially human. If a thought of love, or a gleam of the intellect; a word of justice, an act of pity, a desire for pardon or sacrifice; if a gesture of sympathy, a craving of one's whole being for beauty, goodness, or truth—if emotions like these could affect the universe as they affect the man who has known them, they would call forth miraculous flowery, supernatural radiance, inconceivable melody; they would scatter the night, recall spring and the sunshine, stay the hand of sickness, grief, disaster and misery; gladness would spring from them, and youth be restored; while the mind would gain freedom, thought immortality, and life be eternal. No resistance could check them; their reward would follow as visibly as it follows the labourer's toil, the nightingale's song, or the work of the bee. But we have learned at last that the moral world is a world wherein man is alone; a world contained in ourselves that bears no relation to matter, upon which its influence is only of the most exceptional and hazardous kind. But none the less real, therefore, is this world, or less infinite: and if words break down when they try to tell of it, the reason is only that words, after all, are mere fragments of matter, that seek to enter a sphere where matter holds no dominion. The images that words evoke are for ever betraying the thoughts for which they stand. When we try to express perfect joy, a noble, spiritual ecstasy, a profound, everlasting love, our words can only compare them with animal passion, with drunkenness, brutal and coarse desire. And not only do they thus degrade the noblest triumphs of the soul of man by likening them to primitive instincts, but they incite us to believe, in spite of ourselves, that the object or feeling compared is less real, less true or substantial, than the type to which it is referred. Herein lies the injustice and weakness of every attempt that is made to give voice to the secrets of men. And yet, be words never so faulty, let us still pay careful heed to the events of this inner world. For of all the events it has lain in our power to meet hitherto, they alone truly are human.

Nor should they be regarded as useless, even though the immense torrent of material forces absorb them, as it absorbs the dew that falls from the pale morning flower. Boundless as the world may be wherein we live, it is yet as hermetically enclosed as a sphere of steel. Nothing can fall outside it, for it has no outside; nor can any atom possibly be lost. Even though our species should perish entirely, the stage through which it has caused certain fragments of matter to pass would remain, notwithstanding all ulterior transformations, an indelible principle and an immortal cause. The formidable, provisional vegetations of the primary epoch, the chaotic and immature monsters of the secondary grounds— Plesiosaurus, Ichthyosaurus, Pterodactyl—these might also regard themselves as vain and ephemeral attempts, ridiculous experiments of a still puerile nature, and conceive that they would leave no mark upon a more harmonious globe. And yet not an effort of theirs has been lost in space. They purified the air, they softened the unbreathable flame of oxygen, they paved the way for the more symmetrical life of those who should follow. If our lungs find in the atmosphere the aliment they need, it is thanks to the inconceivably incoherent forests of arborescent fern. We owe our brains and nerves of to-day to fearful hordes of swimming or flying reptiles. These obeyed the order of their life. They did what they had to do. They modified matter in the fashion prescribed to them. And we, by carrying particles of this same matter to the degree of extraordinary incandescence proper to the thought of man, shall surely establish in the future something that never shall perish.

IV

THE PAST

1

Our past stretches behind us in long perspective. It slumbers on the horizon like a deserted city shrouded in mist. A few peaks mark its boundary, and soar predominant into the air; a few important acts stand out, like towers, some with the light still upon them, others half ruined and slowly decaying beneath the weight of oblivion. The trees are bare, the walls crumble, and shadow slowly steals over all. Everything seems to be dead there, and rigid, save only when memory, slowly decomposing, lights it for an instant with an illusory gleam. But apart from this animation, derived only from our expiring recollections, all would appear to be definitively motionless, immutable for ever, divided from present and future by a river that shall not again be crossed.

In reality it is alive; and, for many of us, endowed with a profounder, more ardent life than either present or future. In reality this dead city is often the hot-bed of our existence; and, in accordance with the spirit in which men return to it, shall some find all their wealth there, and others lose what they have.

2

Our conception of the past has much in common with our conception of love and happiness, destiny, justice, and most of the vague but therefore not less potent spiritual organisms that stand for the mighty forces we obey. Our ideas have been handed down to us ready-made by our predecessors; and even when our second consciousness wakes, and, proud in its conviction that henceforth nothing shall be accepted blindly, proceeds most carefully to investigate these ideas, it will squander its time questioning those that loudly protest their right to be heard, and pay no heed to the others close by, that as yet, perhaps, have said nothing. Nor have we, as a rule, far to go to discover these others. They are in us and of us; they wait for us to address them. They are not idle, notwithstanding their silence. Amid the noise and babble of the crowd they are tranquilly directing a portion of our real life; and, as they are nearer to truth than their self-satisfied sisters, they will often be far more simple, and far more beautiful too.

3

Among the most stubborn of these ready-made ideas are those that preside over our conception of the past, and render it a force as imposing and rigid as destiny; a force that indeed becomes destiny working backwards, with its hand outstretched to the destiny that burrows ahead, to which it transmits the last link of our chains. The one thrusts us back, the other urges us forward, with a like irresistible violence. But the violence of the past is perhaps more terrible and more alarming. One may disbelieve in destiny. It is a god whose onslaught many have never experienced. But no one would dream of denying the oppressiveness of the past. Sooner or later its effect must inevitably be felt. Those even who refuse to admit the intangible will credit the past, which their finger can touch, with all the mystery, the influence, the sovereign intervention whereof they have stripped the powers that they have dethroned; thus rendering it the almost unique and therefore more dreadful god of their depopulated Olympus.

4

The force of the past is indeed one of the heaviest that weigh upon men and incline them to sadness. And yet there is none more docile, more eager to follow the direction we could so readily give, did we but know how best to avail ourselves of this docility. In reality, if we think of it, the past belongs to us quite as much as the present, and is far more malleable than the future. Like the present, and to a much greater extent than the future, its existence is all in our thoughts, and our hand controls it; nor is this only true of our material past, wherein there are ruins that we perhaps can restore; it is true also of the regions that are closed to our tardy desire for atonement; it is true above all of our moral past, and of what we consider to be most irreparable there.

5

"The past is past," we say, and it is false; the past is always present. "We have to bear the burden of our past," we sigh, and it is false; the past bears our burden. "Nothing can wipe out the past," and it is false; the least effort of will sends present and future travelling over the past to efface whatever we bid them efface. "The indestructible, irreparable, immutable past!" And that is no truer than the rest. In those who speak thus it is the present that is immutable, and knows not how to repair. "My past is wicked, it is sorrowful, empty," we say again; "as I look back I can see no moment of beauty, of happiness or love; I see nothing but wretched ruins . . ." And that is false; for you see precisely what you yourself place there at the moment your eyes upon it.

6

Our past depends entirely upon our present, and is constantly changing with it. Our past is contained in our memory; and this memory of ours, that feeds on our heart and brain, and is incessantly swayed by them, is the most variable thing in the world, the least independent, the most impressionable. Our chief concern with the past, that which truly remains and forms part of us, is not what we have done, or the adventures that we have met with, but the moral reactions bygone events are producing within us at this very moment, the inward being they have helped to form; and these reactions, that give birth to our sovereign, intimate being, are wholly governed by the manner in which we regard past events, and vary as the moral substance varies that they encounter within us. But with every step in advance that our feelings or intellect take, a change will come in this moral substance; and then, on the instant, the most immutable facts, that seemed to be graven for ever on the stone and bronze of the past, will assume an entirely different aspect, will return to life and leap into movement, bringing us vaster and more courageous counsels, dragging memory aloft with them in their ascent; and what was once a mass of ruin, mouldering in the darkness, becomes a populous city whereon the sun shines again.

7

We have an arbitrary fashion of establishing a certain

number of events behind us. We relegate them to the horizon of our memory; and having set them there, we tell ourselves that they form part of a world in which the united efforts of all mankind could not wipe away a tear, or cause a flower to lift its head. And yet, while admitting that these events have passed beyond our control, we still, with the most curious inconsistency, believe that they have full control over us; whereas the truth is that they can only act upon us to the extent in which we have renounced our right to act upon them. The past asserts itself only in those whose moral growth has ceased; then, and not till then, does it become redoubtable. From that moment we have indeed the irreparable behind us, and the weight of what we have done lies heavy upon our shoulders. But so long as the life of our mind and character flows uninterruptedly on, so long will the past remain in suspense above us; and, as the glance may be that we send towards it, will it, complaisant as the clouds Hamlet showed to Polonius, adopt the shape of the hope or fear, the peace or disquiet, that we are perfecting within us.

8

No sooner has our moral activity weakened than accomplished events rush forward and assail us; and woe to him who opens the door, and permits them to take possession of his hearth! Each one will vie with the other in overwhelming him with the gifts best calculated to shatter his courage. It matters not whether our past has been happy and noble, or lugubrious and criminal, there shall still be great danger in allowing it to enter, not as an invited guest, but like a parasite settling upon us. The result will be either sterile regret or impotent remorse; and remorse and regrets of this kind are equally disastrous. In order to draw from the past what is precious within it—and most of our wealth is there— we must go to it at the hour when we are strongest, most conscious of mastery; enter its domain, and there make choice of what we require, discarding the rest, and laying our command upon it never to cross our threshold without our order. Like all things that only can live at the cost of our spiritual strength, it will soon learn to obey. At first, perhaps, it will endeavour to resist. It will have recourse to artifice and prayer. It will try to tempt us, to cajole. It will drag forward frustrated hopes and joys that are gone for ever, broken affections, well-merited reproaches, expiring hatred and love that is dead, squandered faith and perished beauty; it will thrust before us all that once had been the marvellous essence of our ardour for life; it will point to the beckoning sorrows, decaying happiness, that now haunt the ruin. But we shall pass by, without turning our head; our hand shall scatter the crowd of memories, even as the sage Ulysses, in the Cimmerian night, with his sword prevented the shades— even that of his mother, whom it was not his mission to question—from approaching the black blood that would for an instant have given them life and speech. We shall go straight to the joy, the regret or remorse, whose counsel we need; or to the act of injustice we wish scrupulously to examine, in order either to make reparation, if such still be possible, or that the sight of the wrong we did, whose victims have ceased to be, is required to give us the indispensable force that shall lift us above the injustice it still lies in us to commit.

9

Yes, even though our past contain crimes that now are beyond the reach of our best endeavours, even then, if we consider the circumstances of time and place, and the vast plane of each human existence, these crimes fade out of our life the moment we feel that no temptation, no power on earth, could ever induce us to commit the like again. The world has not forgiven—there is but little that the external sphere will forget or forgive—and their material effects will continue, for the laws of cause and effect differ from those which govern our consciousness. At the tribunal of our personal justice, however—the only tribunal which has decisive action on our inaccessible life, as it is the only one whose decrees we cannot evade, whose concrete judgments stir us to our very marrow—the evil action that we regard from a loftier plane than that at which it was committed, becomes an action that no longer exists for us save in so far as it may serve in the future to render our fall more difficult; nor has it the right to lift its head again except at the moment when we incline once more towards the abyss it guards.

Bitter, surely, must be the grief of him in whose past there are acts of injustice whereof every avenue now is closed, who is no longer able to seek out his victims, and raise them and comfort them. To have abused one's strength in order to despoil some feeble creature who has definitely succumbed beneath the blow; to have callously thrust suffering upon a loving heart, or merely misunderstood and passed by a touching affection that offered itself—these things must of necessity weigh heavily upon our life, and induce a sorrow within us that shall not readily be forgotten. But it depends on the actual point our consciousness has attained whether our entire moral destiny shall be depressed or lifted beneath this burden. Our actions rarely die: and many unjust deeds of ours will therefore inevitably return to life some day to claim their due and start legitimate reprisals. They will find our external life without defence; but before they can reach the inward being at the centre of that life, they must first listen to the judgment we have already passed on ourselves; and in accordance with the nature of that judgment will the attitude be of these mysterious envoys, who have come from the depths where cause and effect are poised in eternal equilibrium. If it has indeed been from the heights of our newly acquired consciousness that we have questioned ourselves, and condemned, they will not be menacing justiciaries whom we shall suddenly see surging in from all sides, but benevolent visitors, friends we have almost expected, and they will draw near us in silence. They know in advance that the man before them is no longer the guilty creature they sought; and instead of bringing hatred, revolt, and despair, or punishments that degrade and kill, they will come charged with ennobling, consoling and purifying thought and penance.

10

The things which differentiate the happy and strong from those who weep and will not be consoled, all derive from the one same principle of confidence and ardour; and thus it is that the manner in which we are able to recall what we have done or suffered is far more important than our actual sufferings or deeds. No past, viewed by itself, can seem happy; and the privileged of fate, who reflect on what remains of the happy years that have flown, have perhaps more reason for sorrow than the unfortunate ones who brood over the dregs of a life of wretchedness. Whatever was one day and has now ceased to be, makes for sadness; above all, whatever was very happy and very beautiful. The object of our regrets—whether these revolve around what has been or might have been—is therefore more or less the same for all men, and their sorrow should be the same. It is not, however; in one case it will reign uninterruptedly, whereas in another it will only appear at very long intervals. It must therefore depend on things other than accomplished facts. It depends on the manner in which men will deal with these facts. The conquerors in this world—those who waste no time setting up an imaginary irreparable and immutable athwart their horizon, those who seem to be born afresh every morning in a world that for ever awakes anew to the future—these know instinctively that what appears to exist no longer is still existing intact, that what appeared to be ended is only completing itself. They know that the years time has taken from them are still in travail; still, under their new master, obeying the old. They know that their past is for ever in movement; that the yesterday which was despondent, decrepit and criminal, will return full of joyousness, innocence, youth, in the track of to-morrow. They know that their image is not yet stamped on the days that are gone; that a decisive deed, or thought, will suffice to break down the whole edifice; that however remote or vast the shadow may be that stretches behind them, they have only to put forth a gesture of gladness or hope for the shadow at once to copy this gesture, and, flashing it back to the remotest, tiniest ruins of early childhood even, to extract unexpected treasure from all this wreckage. They know that they have retrospective action on all bygone deeds; and that the dead themselves will annul their verdicts in order to judge afresh a past that to-day has transfigured and endowed with new life.

They are fortunate who find this instinct in the folds of their cradle. But may the others not imitate it who have it not; and is not human wisdom charged to teach us how we may acquire the salutary instincts that nature has withheld?

11

Let us not lull ourselves to sleep in our past; and if we find that it tends to spread like a vault over our life, instead of incessantly changing beneath our eye; if the present grow into the habit of visiting it, not like a good workman repairing thither to execute the labours imposed upon him by the commands of to-day, but as a too passive, too credulous pilgrim, content idly to contemplate beautiful, motionless ruins—then, the more glorious, the happier that our past may have been, with all the more suspicion should it be regarded by us.

Nor should we yield to the instinct that bids us accord it profound respect, if this respect induce the fear in us that we may disturb its nice equilibrium. Better the ordinary past, content with its befitting place in the shadow, than the sumptuous past which claims to govern what has travelled beyond its reach. Better a mediocre but living present, which acts as though it were alone in the world, than a present which proudly expires in the chains of a marvellous long ago. A single step that we take at this hour towards an uncertain goal, is far more important to us than the thousand leagues we covered in our march towards a dazzling triumph in the days that were. Our past had no other mission than to lift us to the moment at which we are, and there equip us with the needful experience and weapons, the needful thought and gladness. If, at this precise moment, it take from us and divert to itself one particle of our energy, then, however glorious it may have been, it still was useless, and had better never have been. If we allow it to arrest a gesture that we were about to make, then is our death beginning; and the edifices of the future will suddenly take the semblance of tombs.

More dangerous still than the past of happiness and glory is the one inhabited by overpowering and too dearly cherished phantoms. Many an existence perishes in the coils of a fond recollection. And yet, were the dead to return to this earth, they would say, I fancy, with the wisdom that must be theirs who have seen what the ephemeral light still hides from us: "Dry your eyes. There comes to us no comfort from your tears: exhausting you, they exhaust us also. Detach yourself from us, banish us from your thoughts, until such time as you can think of us without strewing tears on the life we still live in you. We endure only in your recollection; but you err in believing that your regrets alone can touch us. It is the things you do that prove to us we are not forgotten, and rejoice our manes; and this without your knowing it, without any necessity that you should turn towards us. Each time that our pale image saddens your ardour, we feel ourselves die anew, and it is a more perceptible, irrevocable death than was our other; bending too often over our tombs, you rob us of the life, the courage and love that you imagine you restore.

"It is in you that we are, it is in all your life that our life resides; and as you become greater, even while forgetting us, so do we become greater too, and our shades draw the deep breath of prisoners whose prison door is flung open.

"If there be anything new we have learned in the world where we are now, it is, first of all, that the good we did to you when we were, like yourselves, on the earth, does not balance the evil wrought by a memory which saps the force and the confidence of life."

12

Above all, let us envy the past of no man. Our own past was created by ourselves, and for ourselves alone. No other could have suited us, no other could have taught us the truth that it alone can teach, or given the strength that it alone can give. And whether it be good or bad, sombre or radiant, it still remains a collection of unique masterpieces the value of which is known to none but ourselves; and no foreign masterpiece could equal the action we have accomplished, the kiss we received, the thing of beauty that moved us so deeply, the suffering we underwent, the anguish that held us enchained, the love that wreathed us in smiles or in tears. Our past is ourselves, what we are and shall be; and upon this unknown sphere there moves no creature, from the happiest down to the most unfortunate, who could foretell how great a loss would be his could he substitute the trace of another for the trace which he himself must leave in life. Our past is our secret, promulgated by the voice of years; it is the most mysterious image of our being, over which Time keeps watch. This image is not dead; a mere nothing degrades or adorns it; it can still grow bright or sombre, can still smile or weep, express love or hatred; and yet it remains recognisable for ever in the midst of the myriad images that surround it. It stands for what we once were, as our aspirations and hopes stand for what we shall be; and the two faces blend, that they may teach us what we are.

Let us not envy the facts of the past, but rather the spiritual garment that the recollection of days long gone will weave around the sage. And though this garment be woven of joy or of sorrow, though it be drawn from the dearth of events or from their abundance, it shall still be equally precious; and those who may see it shining over a life shall not be able to tell whether its quickening jewels and stars were found amid the grudging cinders of a cabin or upon the steps of a palace.

No past can be empty or squalid, no events can be wretched: the wretchedness lies in our manner of welcoming them. And if it were true that nothing had happened to you, that would be the most remarkable adventure that any man ever had met with; and no less remarkable would be the light it would shed upon you. In reality the facts, the opportunities and possibilities, the passions, that await and invite the majority of men, are all more or less the same. Some may be more dazzling than others; their attendant circumstances may differ, but they differ far less than the inward reactions that follow; and the insignificant, incomplete event that falls on a fertile heart and brain will readily attain the moral proportions and grandeur of an analogous incident which, on another plane, will convulse a people.

He who should see, spread out before him, the past lives of a multitude of men, could not easily decide which past he himself would wish to have lived were he not able at the same time to witness the moral results of these dissimilar and unsymmetrical facts. He might not impossibly make a fatal blunder; he might choose an existence overflowing with incomparable happiness and victory, that sparkle like wonderful jewels; while his glance might travel indifferently over a life that appeared to be empty whereas it was truly steeped to the brim in serene emotions and lofty, redeeming thoughts whereby, though the eye saw nothing, that life was yet rendered happy among all. For we are well aware that what destiny has given, and what destiny holds in reserve, can be revolutionised as utterly by thought as by great victory or great defeat. Thought is silent; it disturbs not a pebble on the illusory road we see; but at the crossway of the more actual road that our secret life follows will it tranquilly erect an indestructible pyramid; and thereupon, suddenly, every event, to the very phenomena of earth and heaven, will assume a new direction.

In Siegfried's life, it is not the moment when he forges the prodigious sword that is most important, or when he kills the dragon and compels the gods from his path, or even the dazzling second when he encounters love on the flaming mountain, but indeed the brief instant wrested from eternal decrees, the little childish gesture, when one of his hands, red with the blood of his mysterious victim, having chanced to draw near his lips, his eyes and ears are suddenly opened; he understands the hidden language of all that surrounds him, detects the treachery of the dwarf who represents the powers of evil, and learns in a flash to do that which had to be done.

V

LUCK

1

Once upon a time, an old Servian legend tells us, there were two brothers of whom one was industrious, but unfortunate, and the other lazy, but overwhelmingly prosperous. One day the unfortunate brother meets a beautiful girl who is tending sheep and weaving a golden thread. "To whom do these sheep belong?" he asks. "They belong to whom I belong." "And to whom do you belong?" "To your brother: I am his luck." "And where is my luck then?" "Very far from here." "Can I find it?" "Yes, if you look for it."

So he wanders away in search of his luck. And one evening, in a great forest, he comes across a poor old woman asleep under a tree. He wakes her and asks who she is. "Don't you know me?" she answers. "It is true you never have seen me: I am your luck." "And who can have given me so wretched a luck?" "Destiny." "Can I find destiny?" "Yes, if you look long enough."

So he goes off in search of destiny. He travels a very long time, and at last she is pointed out to him. She lives in an enormous and luxurious palace; but her wealth is dwindling day by day, and the doors and windows of her abode are shrinking. She explains to him that she passes thus, alternately, from misery to opulence; and that her situation at a given moment determines the future of all the children who may come into the world at that moment. "You were born," she says, "when my prosperity was on the wane; and that is the cause of your ill-luck." The only way, she tells him, to hoodwink or get the better of fortune would be to substitute the luck of Militza, his niece, for his own, seeing that she was born at a propitious period. All he need do, she says, is to take this niece into his house, and to declare to any one who may ask him that all he has belongs to Militza.

He does as she bids him, and his affairs at once take a new turn. His herds multiply and grow fat, his trees are bent beneath the masses of fruit, unexpected inheritances come in, his land bears prodigious crops. But one morning, as he stands there, his heart filled with happiness, eyeing a magnificent cornfield, a stranger asks him who the owner may be of these wonderful ears of wheat that, as they sway to and fro beneath the dew, seem twice as heavy and twice as high as the ears in the adjoining field. He forgets himself, and answers, "They are mine." At that very instant fire breaks out in the opposite end of the field, and commences its ravages. Then he remembers the advice that he has neglected to follow: he runs after the stranger shouting, "Stop, come back: I made a mistake: what I told you was not true! This field is not mine: it belongs to my niece Militza!" And the flames have no sooner heard than they suddenly fall away, and the corn shoots up afresh.

2

This naive and very ancient image, which might almost serve to-day as an illustration of our actual ignorance, proves that the mysterious problem of chance has not changed, from the time of man's first questioning glance. We have our thoughts, which build up our intimate happiness or sorrow; and upon this events from without have more or less influence. In some men these thoughts will have acquired such strength, such vigilance, that without their consent nothing can enter the structure of crystal and brass, they have been able to raise on the hill that commands the wonted road of adventures. And we have our will, which our thoughts feed and sustain; and many useless or harmful events can be held in check by our will. But around these islets, within which is a certain degree of safety, of immunity from attack, extends a region as vast and uncontrollable as the ocean, a region swayed by chance as the waves are swayed by the wind. Neither will nor thought can keep one of these waves from suddenly breaking upon us; and we shall be caught unawares, and perhaps be wounded and stunned. Only when the wave has retreated can thought and will begin their beneficent action. Then they will raise us, and bind up our wounds; restore animation, and take careful heed that the mischief the shock has wrought shall not reach the profound sources of life. Their mission extends no further, and may, on the surface, appear very humble. In reality, however, unless chance assume the irresistible form of cruel disease or death, the workings of will and thought are sufficient to neutralise all its efforts, and to preserve what is best and most essential to man in human happiness.

3

Redoubtable, multitudinous chance is for ever threading its watchful way through the midst of the events we have foreseen, and round and about our most deliberate actions, wherewith we are slowly tracing the broad lines of our existence. The air we breathe, the time we traverse, the space through which we move, are all peopled by lurking circumstances, which pick us out from among the crowd. The least study of their habits will quickly convince us that these strange daughters of hazard, who should be blind and deaf as their father, by no means act in his irresponsible fashion. They are well aware of what they are doing, and rarely make a mistake. With inexplicable certainty do they move to the passer-by whom they have been sent to confront, and lightly touch his shoulder. Two men may be travelling upon the same road, and at the same hour; but there will be no hesitation or doubt in the ranks of the double, invisible troop whom fortune has ambushed there. Towards one a band of white virgins will hasten, bearing palms and amphorae, presenting the thousand unexpected delights of the journey; as the other approaches, the "Evil Women," whom Aeschylus tells of, will hurl themselves from the hedges, as though they were charged to avenge, upon this unwitting victim, some inexpiable crime committed by him before he was born.

4

There is scarcely one of us who has not been able, in some measure, to follow the workings of destiny in life. We have all known men who met with a prosperity or disaster entirely out of relation to any of their actions; men upon whom good or bad luck seemed suddenly, at a turn of the road, to spring from the ground or descend from the stars, undeserved, unprovoked, but complete and inevitable. One, we will say, who scarcely has given a thought to some appointment for which he knows his rival to be better equipped, will see this rival vanish at the decisive moment, another, who has counted upon the protection of a most influential friend, will see this friend die on the very day when his assistance could be of value. A third, who has neither talent nor beauty, will arrive each morning at the Palace of Fortune, Glory or Love at the brief instant when every door lies open; while another, a man of great merit, who long has pondered the legitimate step he is taking, presents himself at the hour when ill-luck shall have closed the gate for the next half-century. One man will risk his health twenty times in imbecile feats, and never experience the least ill-effect; another will deliberately venture it in an honourable cause, and lose it without hope of return. To help the first, thousands of unknown people, who never have seen him, will be obscurely working; to hinder the second, thousands of unknown people labour, who are ignorant of his existence. And all, on the one side as well as the other, are totally unaware of what they are doing; they obey the same minute, widely-distributed order; and at the prescribed moment the detached pieces of the mysterious machine join, dovetail, unite; and we have two complete and dissimilar destinies set into motion by Time.

In a curious book on "Chance and Destiny," Dr. Foissac gives various strange examples of the persistent, inexplicable, fundamental, pre-ordained, irreducible iniquity in which many existences are steeped. As we go through page after page, we feel almost as though we were being conducted through the disconcerting laboratories of another world where, in the absence of every instrument that human justice and reason might hold indispensable, happiness and sorrow are being parcelled out and allotted. Take, for instance, the life of Vauvenargues, one of the most admirable of men, and certainly, of all the great sages, the most unfortunate. Whenever his fortune hangs in the balance, he is attacked and prostrated by cruel disease; and notwithstanding the efforts of his genius, his bravery, his moral beauty, day after day he is wantonly betrayed or falls victim to gratuitous injustice; and at the age of thirty-two he dies, at the very moment when recognition is at last awaiting his work. So too there is the terrible story of Lesurques,[1] in which we see a

Maurice Maeterlinck

thousand coincidences that might have been contrived in hell, blending and joining together to work the ruin of an innocent man; while truth, chained down by fate, dumbly shrieking, as we do when wrestling with nightmare, is unable to put forth a single gesture that shall rend the veil of night. There is Aimar de Ransonnet, President of the Parliament of Paris, one of the most upright of men, who first of all is suddenly dismissed from his office, sees his daughter die on a dunghill before his eyes, his son perish at the hands of the executioner, and his wife struck by lightning; while he himself is accused of heresy and sent to the Bastille, where he dies of grief before he is brought to trial.

The calamities that befell Oedipus and the Atrides are regarded by us as improbable and fabulous; and yet we find in contemporary history that fatality clings with no less persistence to families such as the Stuarts, the Colignys,[2] &c., and hounds to their death, with what almost seems personal vindictiveness, pitiable and innocent victims like Henrietta of England, daughter of Henry IV., Louise de Bourbon, Joseph II., and Marie-Antoinette.

And again in another category, what shall we say of the injustice—unintelligent but apparently almost conscious, almost systematic and premeditated—of games of chance, duels, battles, storms, shipwrecks, and fires? Or of the inconceivable luck of a Chastenet de Puysegur who, after forty years' service, in the course of which he took part in thirty battles and a hundred and twenty sieges, always in the front rank and displaying the most romantic courage, was never once touched by shot or steel, while Marshal Oudinot was wounded thirty-five times, and General Trezel was struck by a bullet in every encounter? What shall we say of the extraordinary fortune of Lauzun, Chamillart, Casanova, Chesterfield, &c., or of the inconceivable, unvarying prosperity that attended the crimes of Sylla, Marius, or

Dionysius the Elder, who, in his extreme old age, after an odious but fantastically successful life, died of joy on learning that the Athenians had just crowned one of his tragedies? Or, finally, of Herod, surnamed the Great or the Ascalonite, who swam in blood, murdered one of his wives and five of his children, put to death every upright man who might chance to offend him, and yet was fortunate in all his undertakings?

6

These famous examples, which might be indefinitely multiplied, are in truth no more than the abnormal and historic presentments of what is shown to us every day, in a humbler but not less emphatic fashion, by the thousand and one caprices of propitious or contrary fortune at work on the small and ill-lit stage of ordinary life.

Doubtless, we must, first of all, when closely examining such insolent prosperity or unvarying disaster, attribute a royal share to the physical or moral causes which are capable of explaining them. Had we ourselves known Vauvenargues, we should probably have detected a certain timidity, irresolution or misplaced pride in his character whereby he was disabled from allowing the opportunity to mature or from seizing it with sufficient vigour. And Lesurques, it may be, was deficient in ability, in one knows not what, in that prodigious personal force that one expects to find in falsely-accused innocence. Nor can it be denied that the Stuarts, no less than Joseph II. and Marie-Antoinette, were guilty of enormous blunders that invited disaster; or that Lauzun, Casanova, and Lord Chesterfield had flung to the winds those essential scruples that hinder the honest man. So too is it certain that although the existence of Sylla, Marius, Dionysius the Elder, and Herod the Ascalonite may have been externally almost incomparably fortunate, few men, I fancy, would care to have lurking within them the strange, restless, blood-stained phantom, possessed neither of thought nor of feeling, on which the happiness must depend (if the word happiness be indeed applicable here) that is founded upon unceasing crime. But, this deduction being made, and on the most reasonable, most liberal scale (which will become the more generous as we see more of life and understand it better, and penetrate further into the secrets of little causes and great effects), we shall still be forced to admit that there remains, in these obstinately recurring coincidences, in these indissoluble series of good or evil fortune, these persistent runs of good or bad luck, a considerable, often essential, and sometimes exclusive share that can be ascribed only to the impenetrable, incontrovertible will of a real but unknown power; which is known as Chance, Fatality, Destiny, Luck, Fortune, good or evil Star, Angel with the White Wings, Angel with the Black Wings, and by many other names, that vary in accordance with the more or less imaginative, more or less poetic genius of centuries and peoples. And here we have one of the most serious, most perplexing problems of all those that have to be solved by man before he may legitimately regard himself as the principal, independent and irrevocable inhabitant of this earth.

7

Let us reduce the problem to its simplest terms, and submit it to our reason. First, however, let us consider whether it affects man alone. We have with us, upon this curiously incomprehensible globe, silent and faithful companions of our existence; and we shall often find it helpful to let our eyes rest upon these when, having reached certain altitudes that perhaps are illusory, giddiness seizes our brain and inclines us too readily to the idea that the stars, the gods or the veiled representatives of the sublime laws of the universe, are concerned solely with us. These poor brothers of our animal life, that are so calmly, so confidently resigned, would appear to know many things that we have forgotten; they are the tranquil custodians of the secret that we seek so anxiously. It is evident that animals, and notably domestic animals, have also a kind of destiny. They too know what prolonged and gratuitous happiness means; they also have encountered the persistent misfortune for which no cause can be found. They have the same right as we to speak of their star, their good or bad luck, their prosperity or disaster. Compare the fate of the cab-horse, that ends its days at the knacker's, after having passed through the hands of a hundred brutal and nameless masters, with that of the thorough-bred which dies of old age in the stable of a kind-hearted master; and from the point of view of justice (unless we accept the Buddhist theory, that life in this world is the reward or punishment of an anterior existence) explanation is as completely lacking as in the case of the man whom chance has reduced to poverty or raised to wealth. There is, in Flanders, a breed of draught-dogs upon which destiny alternately lavishes her favour and her spite. Some will be bought by a butcher, and lead a magnificent life. The work is trifling: in the morning, harnessed four abreast, they draw a light cart to the slaughter-house, and at night, galloping joyously, triumphantly, home through the narrow streets of the ancient towns with their tiny, lit-up gables, bring it back, overflowing with meat. Between-times there is leisure, and marvellous leisure, among the rats and the waste of the slaughter-house. They are copiously fed, they are fat, they shine like seals, and taste in its fulness the only happiness dreamed of by the simple and ferreting instinct of the honest dog. But their unfortunate brethren of the same litter, that the lame sand-pedlar buys, or the old collector of household refuse, or the needy peasant with his great, cruel clogs—

these are chained to heavy carts or shapeless barrows; they are filthy, mangy, hairless, emaciated, starving; and follow till they die the circles of a hell into which they were thrust by a few coppers dropped into some horny palm. And, in a world less directly subject to man, there must evidently be partridges, pheasants, deer, hares, which have no luck, which never escape the gun; while others, one knows not how or why, emerge unscathed from every battue.

They, therefore, are exposed, like ourselves, to incontestable injustice. But it does not occur to us, when considering their hardships, to set all the gods in motion or seek explanation from the mysterious powers; and yet what happens to them may well be no more than the image, naively simplified, of what happens to us. It is true that we play the precise part, in their case, of those mysterious powers whom we seek in our own. But what right have we to expect from these last more consciousness, more intelligent justice, than we ourselves show in our dealings with animals? And in any event, if this instance shall only have deprived chance of a little of its useless prestige and have proportionately augmented our spirit of initiative and struggle, there will be a gain the importance of which is by no means to be despised.

8

Still further allowance must therefore be made; but yet there undoubtedly remains—at least as far as the more complex life of man is concerned—a cause of good or evil fortune as yet untouched by our explanations, in the often visible will of chance, which one might almost call the "small change" of fatality. We know—and this is one of those formless but fundamental ideas on the laws of life that the experience of thousands of years has turned into a kind of instinct—we know that men exist who, other things being equal, are "lucky" or "unlucky." Circumstances permitted me to follow very closely the career of a friend of mine who was dogged by persistent ill-fortune. I do not mean to imply by this that his life was unhappy. It is even remarkable that the malign influences always respected the broad lines of his veritable happiness; probably because these were well guarded. For he had in him a strong moral existence, profound thoughts and hopes, feelings and convictions. He was well aware that these were possessions that fortune could not touch: which indeed could not be destroyed without his consent. Destiny is not invincible; through life's very centre runs a great inward canal, which we have the power to turn towards happiness or sorrow; although its ramifications, that extend over our days, and the thousand tributaries that flow in from external hazards, are all independent of our will.

It is thus that a beautiful river, streaming down from the heights and ashine with magnificent glaciers, passes at length through plains and through cities, whence it receives only poisonous water. For an instant the river is troubled; and we fear lest it lose, and never recover again, the image of the pure blue sky that the crystal fountains had lent: the image that seemed its soul, and the deep and the limpid expression of its great strength. But if we rejoin it, down yonder, beneath those great trees, we shall find that it has already forgotten the foulness of the gutters. It has caught the azure again in its transparent waves; and flows on to the sea, as clear as it was on the days when it first smilingly leapt from its source on the mountains.

And so, as regards this friend of mine, although forced more than once to shed tears, they were at least not of the kind that memory never forgets, not of those that fall from our eyes as we mourn our own death. Every failure, the inevitable disappointment once over, served only in effect to knit him the closer to his secret happiness, to affirm this within him, and draw a more sombre outline around it, that it might thereby appear the more precious, and ardent, and certain. But no sooner had he quitted this charmed enclosure than hostile incidents vied with each other in their attacks upon him. As for instance—he was a very good fencer: he had three duels, and was wounded each time by a less skilful adversary. If he went on board ship, the voyage would rarely be prosperous. Whatever undertaking he put money into was sure to turn out badly. A judicial error, into which a whole series of curiously malevolent circumstances dragged him, was productive of long and serious trouble. Further, although his face was agreeable, and the expression of his eyes loyal and frank, he was not what one calls "sympathetic": he did not arouse at first sight that spontaneous affection which we often give, without knowing why, to the unknown who passes, to an enemy even. Nor was he more fortunate in his affections. Of a loving disposition, and infinitely worthier of being loved than most of those to whom he was sacrificed by the chance-governed heart of women—here again he met with nothing but treachery, deceit and sorrow. He went his way, extricating himself as best he could from the paltry snares that malicious fortune prepared at every step; nor was he discouraged or deeply saddened, only somewhat surprised at so strange a persistence; until at last there came the great and solitary good fortune of his life: a love that was the complement of the one that was eager within him, a love that was complete, passionate, exclusive, unalterable. And from that moment it was as though he had come under the influence of another star, the beneficent rays of which were blending with his own; vexatious events grew slowly remoter, fewer, warier of attacking him, tardier in their approach. They seemed reluctantly to abandon their habit of selecting him as their victim. He actually saw his *luck turn.* And now that he has gone back, as it were, into the indifferent and neutral atmosphere of chance common to most men, he smiles when he remembers the time when every gesture of his was watched by the invisible enemy, and aroused a danger.

9

Let us not look to the gods for an explanation of these phenomena. Until these gods shall have clearly explained themselves, there is nothing that they can explain for us. And destiny, which is merely the god of which we know least, has less right than any of the others to intervene and cry to us, as it does from the depths of its inscrutable night: "It is I who so willed it!" Nor let us invoke the illimitable laws of the universe, the intentions of history, the will of the worlds, the justice of the stars. These powers exist: we submit to them, as we submit to the might of the sun. But they act without knowing us; and within the wide circle of their influence a liberty remains to us still that is probably immense. They have better work on hand than to be for ever bending over us to lift a blade of grass or drop a leaf in the little paths of our anthill. Since we ourselves are here the parties concerned, it is, I imagine, within ourselves that the key of the mystery shall be found; for it is probable that every creature carries within him the best solution of the problem that he presents. Within us, underlying the conscious existence that our reason and will control, is a profounder existence, one side of which connects with a past beyond the record of history, the other with a future that thousands of years cannot exhaust. We may safely conceive that all the gods lie hidden within it; that those wherewith we have peopled the earth and the planets will emerge one by one, in order to give it a name and a form that our imagination may understand. And as man's vision grows clearer, as he shows less desire for image and symbol, so will the number of these names, the number of these forms, tend to diminish. He will slowly arrive at the stage when there shall be one only that he will proclaim, or reserve; when it shall be revealed to him that this last form, this last name, is truly no more than the last image of a power whose throne was always within him. Then will the gods that had gone forth from us be found again in ourselves; and it is there that we will question them to-day.

10

I hold therefore that it is in this unconscious life of ours, in this existence that is so vast, so divine, so inexhaustible and unfathomable, that we must seek for the explanation of fortunate or contrary chances. Within us is a being that is our veritable ego, our first-born: immemorial, illimitable, universal, and probably immortal. Our intellect, which is merely a kind of phosphorescence that plays on this inner sea, has as yet but faint knowledge of it. But our intellect is gradually learning that every secret of the human phenomena it has hitherto not understood must reside there, and there alone. This unconscious being lives on another plane than our intellect, in another world. It knows nothing of Time and Space, the two formidable but illusory walls between which our reason must flow if it would not be hopelessly lost. It knows no proximity, it knows no distance; past and future concern it not, or the resistance of matter. It is familiar with all things; there is nothing it cannot do. To this power, this knowledge, we have indeed at all times accorded a certain varying recognition; we have given names to its manifestations, we have called them instinct, soul, unconsciousness, sub-consciousness, reflex action, presentiment, intuition, &c. We credit it more especially with the indeterminate and often prodigious force contained in those of our nerves that do not directly serve to produce our will and our reason: a force that would appear to be the very fluid of life. Its nature is probably more or less the same in all men; but it has very different methods of communicating with the intellect. In some men this unknown principle is enshrined at so great a depth that it concerns itself solely with physical functions and the permanence of the species; whereas in others it would seem to be for ever on the alert, rising again and again to the surface of external and conscious life, which its fairy-like presence quickens; intervening at every instant, warning, deciding, counselling; blending with most of the essential facts of a career. Whence comes this faculty? There are no fixed or certain laws. We do not detect, for instance, any constant relation between the activity of the unconsciousness and the development of the intellect. This activity obeys rules of which we know nothing. So far as we at present can tell, it would seem to be purely accidental. We discover it in one man, and not in another; nor have we any clue that shall help us to guess at the reason of this difference.

11

The probable course pursued by fortunate or contrary chances may well be as follows. A happy or untoward event, that has sprung from the profound recesses of great and eternal laws, arises before us and completely blocks the way. It stands motionless there: immovable, inevitable, dispropor-tionate. It pays no heed to us; it has not come on our account, but for itself, because of itself. It ignores us completely. It is we who approach the event; we who, having arrived within the sphere of its influence, will either fly from it or face it, try a circuitous route or fare boldly onwards. Let us assume that the event is disastrous: fire, death, disease, or a somewhat abnormal form of accident or calamity. It waits there, invisible, indifferent, blind, but perfect and unalter-able; but as yet it is merely potential. It exists entire, but only in the future; and for us, whose intellect and consciousness are served by senses unable to perceive things otherwise than through the succession of time, it is as though it were not.

Let us be still more precise; let us take the case of a shipwreck. The ship that must perish has not yet left the port; the rock or the shoal that shall rend it sleeps peacefully beneath the waves; the storm that shall burst forth at the end of the month is slumbering, far beyond our gaze, in the secret of the skies. Normally, were nothing written, had the catastrophe[3] not already taken place in the future, fifty passengers would have arrived from five or six different countries, and have duly gone on board. But destiny has clearly marked the vessel for its own. She must most certainly perish. And for months past, perhaps for years, a mysterious selection has been at work amongst the passengers who were to have departed upon the same day. It is possible that out of fifty who had originally intended to sail, only twenty will cross the gangway at the moment of lifting the anchor. It is even possible that not a single one of the fifty will listen to the insistent claims of the circumstance that, but for the disaster ahead, would have rendered their departure imperative, and that their place will be taken by twenty or thirty others in whom the voice of Chance does not speak with a similar power. Here we touch the profoundest depths of the profoundest of human enigmas; and the hypothesis necessarily falters. But is it not more reasonable, in the fictitious case before us—wherein we merely thrust into prominence what is of constant occurrence in the more obscure conjunctures of daily life—to regard both decision and action as emanating from our unconsciousness, rather than from doubtful, and distant, gods? Our unconsciousness is aware of the catastrophe: it must be: our unconsciousness sees it; for it knows neither time nor space, and the disaster is therefore happening as actually before its eyes as before the eyes of the eternal powers. The mode of prescience matters but little. Out of the fifty travellers who have been warned, two or three will have had a real presentiment of the danger; these will be the ones in whom unconsciousness is free and untrammelled, and therefore more readily able to attain the first, and still obscure, layers of intellect. The others suspect nothing: they inveigh against the inexplicable obstacles and delays: they strain every nerve to arrive in time, but their departure becomes impossible. They fall ill, take a wrong road, change their plans, meet with some insignificant adventure, have a quarrel, a love affair, a moment of idleness or forgetfulness, which detains them in spite of themselves. To the first it will never have even occurred to sail on the ill-starred boat, although this be the one that they should logically, inevitably, have been compelled to choose. But the efforts that their unconsciousness has put forth to save them have their workings so deep down that most of these men will have no idea that they owe their life to a fortunate chance; and they will honestly believe that they never intended to sail by the ship that the powers of the sea had claimed.

12

As for those who punctually make their appearance at the fatal tryst, they belong to the tribe of the unlucky. They are the unfortunate race of our race. When the rest all fly, they alone remain in their places. When others retreat, they advance boldly. They infallibly travel by the train that shall leave the rails, they pass underneath the tower at the exact moment of its collapse, they enter the house in which the fire is smouldering, cross the forest on which lightning shall fall, entrust all they have to the banker who means to abscond. They love the one woman on earth whom they should have avoided, they make the gesture they should not have made, they do the thing they should not have done. But when fortune beckons and the others are hastening, urged by the deep voice of benevolent powers, these pass by, not hearing; and, vouchsafed no advice or warning but that of their intellect, the very wise old guide whose purblind eyes see

Maurice Maeterlinck

only the tiny paths at the foot of the mountain, they go astray in a world that human reason has not yet understood. These men have surely the right to exclaim against destiny; and yet not on the grounds that they would prefer. They have the right to ask why it has withheld from them the watchful guard who warns their brethren. But, this reproach once made—and it is the cardinal reproach against irreducible injustice—they have no further cause of complaint. The universe is not hostile to them. Calamities do not pursue them; it is they who go towards calamity Things from without wish them no ill; the mischief comes from themselves. The misfortune they meet has not been lying in wait for them; they selected it for their own. With them, as with all men, events are posted along the course of their years, like goods in a bazaar that stand ready for the customer who shall buy them. No one deceives them; they merely deceive themselves. They are in no wise persecuted; but their unconscious soul fails to perform its duty. Is it less adroit than the others: is it less eager? Does it slumber hopelessly in the depths of its secular prison: and can no amount of will-power arouse it from its fatal lethargy, and force the redoubtable doors that lead from the life that unconsciously is aware of all things to the intelligent life that knows nothing?

13

A friend in whose presence I was discussing these matters said to me yesterday: "Life, whose questions are more searching than those of the philosophers, will this very day compel me to add a somewhat curious problem to those you have stated. I am wondering what the result will be when two 'lucks'—in other words, two unconsciousnesses, of which one is adroit and fortunate, the other inept and bungling—meet and in some measure blend in the same venture, the same undertaking? Which will triumph over the other? I soon shall know. This afternoon I propose to take a step that will be of supreme importance to the person I value above all others in this world. Her entire future may almost be said to depend upon it, her exterior happiness, the possibility of her living in accordance with her nature and her rights. Now to me chance has always been a faithful and far-seeing friend; and as I glance over my past, and review the five or six decisive moments which, as with all men, were the golden pivots on which fortune turned, I am induced to believe in my star, and am morally certain that if I alone were concerned in the step I am taking to-day, it would be bound to succeed, because I am 'lucky.' But the person on whose behalf I am acting has never been fortunate. Her intellect is remarkably subtle and profound, her will is a thousand times stronger and better balanced than my own; but, with all this, one can only believe that she possesses a foolish or malignant unconsciousness, which has persistently, ruthlessly, exposed her to act after act of injustice, dishonesty, and treachery, has robbed her again and again of her due, and compelled her to travel the path of disastrous coincidence. Be sure that it would have forced her to embark on the ship that you speak of. I ask myself, therefore, what attitude will my vigilant, thoughtful unconsciousness adopt towards this indolent and sinning brother, in whose name it will have to act, whose place, as it were, it will take?

"How, and where, is the momentous decision being at this moment arrived at, in search of which I shall so soon set forth? What power is it that now, at this very moment, while I am speaking, is balancing the pros and cons, and decreeing the happiness or sorrow of the woman I represent? From which sphere, or perhaps immemorial virtue, from what hidden spirit or invisible star, will the weight fall that shall incline the scale to light or to darkness? To judge by outward appearance, decision must rest with the will, the reason, the interest of the parties engaged; in reality it often is otherwise. When one finds oneself thus face to face with the problem which directly affects a person we love, this problem no longer appears quite so simple; our eyes open wider, and we throw a startled, anxious, in a sense almost a virgin glance, upon all this unknown that leads us and that we are compelled to obey.

"I take this step therefore with more emotion, I put forth more zeal and vigour, than if it were my own life, my own happiness, that stood in peril. She for whom I am acting is indeed 'more I than I am myself,' and for a long time past her happiness has been the source of mine. Of this both my heart and my reason are fully aware; but does my unconsciousness know? My reason and heart, that form my consciousness, are barely thirty years old; my unconscious soul, still reminiscent of primitive secrets, may well date centuries back. Its evolution is very deliberate. It is as slow as a world that turns in time without end. It will probably therefore not yet have learned that a second existence has linked itself to mine, and completely absorbs it. How many years must elapse before the great news shall penetrate to its retreat? Here again we note its diversity, its inequality. In one man, perhaps, unconsciousness will immediately recognise what is taking place in his heart; in another, it will very tardily lend itself to the phenomena of reason. There is a love, again, such as that of the mother for her child, in which it moves in advance of both heart and reason. Only after a very long time does the unconscious soul of a mother separate itself from that of her children; it watches over these at first with far more zeal and solicitude than over the mother. But, in a love like mine, who shall say whether my unconsciousness has gathered that this love is more essential to me than my life? I myself believe that it is satisfied that the step I propose to take in no way concerns me. It will not appear; it will not intervene. At the very moment when I shall be feverishly displaying all the energy I possess, when I shall be striving for victory more keenly than were my salvation at stake, it will be tending its own mysterious affairs deep down in its shadowy dwelling. Were I seeking justice for myself, it would already be on the alert. It would know, perhaps, that I had better do nothing to-day. I should probably have not the slightest idea of intervention; but it would raise some unforeseen obstacle. I should fall ill; catch a bad cold, be prevented by some secondary event from arriving at the unpropitious hour. Then, when I was actually in the presence of the man who held my destiny in his hands, my vigilant friend would spread its wings over me, its breath would inspire me, its light would dispel my darkness. It would dictate to me the words that I must say: they would be the only words that could meet the secret objections of the master of my Fate. It would regulate my attitude, my silence, my gestures; it would endow me with the confidence, the nameless influence, which often will govern the decisions of men far more than the reasons of reason or the eloquence of interest. But here I am sorely afraid that my unconsciousness will do none of these things. It will remain perfectly passive. It will not appear on the familiar threshold. In its obtuseness, impervious to the fact that my life has ceased to be self-contained, it will act in accordance with its ancient traditions, those that have ruled it these hundreds of years; it will persist in regarding this matter as one that does not concern me, and will believe that in helping my failure it will be doing me service; whereas in truth it will afflict me more grievously, cause me more sorrow, than if it were to betray me at the approach of death. I shall be importing, therefore, into this affair, only the palest reflection, a kind of phantom, of my own luck; and I ask myself with dread whether this will suffice to counterbalance the contrary fortune which I have, as it were, assumed, and which I represent."

Maurice Maeterlinck

14

Some days later my friend informed me that his action had been unsuccessful. It may be that this reverse was only due to chance or to his own want of confidence. For the confidence that sees success ahead pursues it with a pertinacity and resource of which hesitation and doubt are incapable; nor is it troubled by any of those involuntary weaknesses which give so great an advantage to the adversary's instinct. And there may probably be much truth also in his manner of depicting unconsciousness. For truly, there are depths in us at which unconsciousness and confidence would seem to blend, and it becomes difficult to say where the first begins, or the second leaves off.

We will not pursue this too subtle inquiry, but rather consider the other and more direct questions that life is ever putting to us concerning one of its greatest problems—chance. This possesses what may be called a daily interest. It asks us, for instance, what attitude we should adopt towards men who are incontestably unlucky; men whose evil star has such pernicious power that it infallibly brings disaster to whatever comes within the range—often a very wide one—of its baleful influence. Ought we unhesitatingly to fly from such men, as Dr. Foissac advises? Yes, doubtless, if their misfortunes arise from an imprudent and unduly hazardous spirit, a heedless, quarrelsome, mischief-making, Utopian or clouded mind. Ill-luck is a contagious disease; and one unconsciousness will often infect another. But if the misfortunes be wholly unmerited, or fall upon those who are dear to us, flight were unjust and shameful. In such a case the conscious side of our being—which, though it know but little, is yet able to fashion truths of a different order, truths that might almost be the first flowers of a dawning world—is bound to resist the universal wisdom of unconsciousness, bound to brave its warnings and involve it in its own ruin, which may well be a victory upon an ideal plane that one day perhaps shall appeal to the unconsciousness also.

15

We ask ourselves, therefore, whether unconsciousness, which we regard as the source of our luck, is really incapable of change or improvement. Have we not all of us noticed how strange are the ways of chance? When we behold it active in a small town, or among a certain number of men within the range of our own observation, the goddess would seem to become as persistent as a gadfly, and no less fantastic. Her very marked personality and character will vary in accordance with the event or being whereon she may fasten. She has all kinds of eccentricities, but pursues each one logically to the finish. Her first gesture will tell us nothing; from her second we can predict all that she means to do. Protean divinity that no image could completely describe, here she leaps suddenly forth, like a fountain in the midst of a desert, to disappear after having given birth to an ephemeral oasis; there she returns at regular intervals, collecting and scattering, like migratory birds that obey the rhythm of the seasons. On our right she fells a man and concerns herself with him no further; on our left she bears down another, and furiously worries her victim. But, though she bring favour or ruin, she will almost always remain astoundingly faithful to the character she has once and for all assumed in a particular case. This man, for instance, who has been unsuccessful in war, will continue to be unsuccessful; that other will invariably win or lose at cards; a third will infallibly be deceived; a fourth will find water, fire, or the dangers of the street especially hostile; a fifth will be constantly fortunate or unfortunate in love, money matters, &c., and so to the end. All this may prove nothing, but we may regard it at least as some indication that her realm is truly within us and not without; and that a hidden force that emanates only from us provides her with form and with vestment.

Her habits at times will suddenly alter, one eccentricity producing another; some brusque change of front will give the lie to her character, to confirm it the instant after in a new atmosphere. We say then that "luck turns." May it not rather be our unconsciousness that is gradually developing, at last displaying some prudence, attention, and slowly becoming aware that important events are stirring in the world to which it is attached? Has it gained some experience? Has a ray of intelligence, a spark of will-power, filtered through to its lair and hinted at danger? Does it learn, after years have flown, and trial after trial has had to be borne, the wisdom of casting aside its confident apathy? Can external disaster arouse it from perilous slumber? Or, if it always has known what was happening over the roof of its prison, is it able, after long and painful effort, at last, at the critical moment, to contrive some sort of crevice in the great wall, built by the indifference of centuries, that separates it from its unknown sisters; and does it thus succeed in entering the ephemeral life on which a part of its own life depends?

16

And yet we must admit that this hypothesis of unconsciousness will not suffice to account for all the injustice of chance. Its three most iniquitous acts are the three disasters—the most terrible of all to which man is exposed—that habitually strike him before birth: I refer to absolute poverty, disease (especially in the shocking forms of physiological degradation and incurable infirmities, of repulsive ugliness and deformity), and intellectual weakness. These are the three great priestesses of unrighteousness that lie in wait for innocence and brand it, on the threshold of life. And yet, mysterious as their method of choice may appear, the triple source whence they derive these three irremediable scourges is less mysterious than one is inclined to believe. We need not look for it in a pre-established will, in fatal, hostile, eternal, impenetrable laws. Poverty has its origin in man's own province; and though we may marvel why one should be rich and the other poor, we are well aware that the existence, side by side, of excessive wealth and excessive misery, is due to human injustice alone. In this wickedness neither gods nor stars have part. And as for disease and mental weakness, when we shall have eliminated from them what now is due to poverty, mother of most of our moral and physical sorrows, as well as to the anterior, and by no means inevitable, faults of the parents, then, though some measure of persistent and unaccountable injustice may still remain, this relic of mystery will very nigh go into the hollow of the philosopher's hand, and there he shall, later, examine it at his leisure. But we of today shall be wise in refusing to allow our life to be unnecessarily darkened, or hedged round with imaginary maledictions and foes.

As far as ordinary luck is concerned, we shall do well to believe, for the moment, that the history of our fortune (which is not necessarily the history of our real happiness, since this may be wholly independent of luck) is the history of our unconscious being. There are more elements of probability in such a creed than in the assumption that the stars, eternity, or the spirit of the universe are taking part in our petty adventures; and it gives more spur to our courage. And this idea—even though it may possibly be as difficult to alter the character of our unconsciousness as to modify the course of Mars or of Venus—still seems less distant and less chimerical than the other; and when we have to choose between two probabilities, it is our imperative duty to select the one that presents the least obstacles to our hopes. Further, should misfortune be indeed inevitable, there would be I know not what proud consolation in being able to tell ourselves that it issues solely from us, and that we are not the victims of a malign will or the playthings of useless chance that in suffering more than our brothers we are perhaps only recording, in time and space, the necessary form of our own personality. And so long as calamity do not attack the intimate pride of man, he retains the force to continue the struggle and accomplish his essential mission: which is, to live with all the ardour whereof he is capable, and as though his life were of greater consequence than any other to the destinies of mankind.

This idea is also more conformable to the vast law which restores to us, one by one, the gods wherewith we had filled the world. Of these gods the greater number were merely the effects of causes that reposed in ourselves. As we progress we shall discover that many a force that mastered us and aroused our wonder was only an ill-understood fragment of our own power; and this will probably become more apparent every day.

And though we shall not have conquered the unknown force by bringing it nearer or enclosing it within us, there yet shall be gain in knowing where it abides and where we may question it. Obscure forces surround us; but the one that concerns us most nearly lies at the very centre of our being. All the others pass through it: it is their trysting-place: they re-enter and congregate there; and only in the degree of their relation to it have they interest for us.

To distinguish this force from the host of others we have called it unconsciousness. And when we shall have succeeded in studying this unconsciousness more closely, when its mysterious adroitness, its antipathies and preference, its helplessness, shall be better known to us, we shall have most strangely blunted the teeth and nails of the monster who persecutes us under the name of Fortune, Destiny or Chance. At the present hour we are feeding it still as a blind man might feed the lion that at last shall devour him. Soon perhaps the lion will be seen by us in its true light, and we shall then learn how to subdue him.

Let us therefore unweariedly follow each path that leads from our consciousness to our unconsciousness. We shall thus succeed in hewing some kind of track through the great and as yet impassable roads that lead from the seen to the unseen, from man to God, from the individual to the universe. At the end of these roads lies hidden the general secret of life. In the meanwhile let us adopt the hypothesis that offers the most encouragement to our existence in this life; in this life which has need of us for the solution of its own enigmas, seeing that in us its secrets crystallise the most limpidly and most rapidly.

THE END

Maurice Maeterlinck

Choose from Thousands of 1stWorldLibrary Classics By

A. M. Barnard
Ada Leverson
Adolphus William Ward
Aesop
Agatha Christie
Alexander Aaronsohn
Alexander Kielland
Alexandre Dumas
Alfred Gatty
Alfred Ollivant
Alice Duer Miller
Alice Turner Curtis
Alice Dunbar
Allen Chapman
Alleyne Ireland
Ambrose Bierce
Amelia E. Barr
Amory H. Bradford
Andrew Lang
Andrew McFarland Davis
Andy Adams
Angela Brazil
Anna Alice Chapin
Anna Sewell
Annie Besant
Annie Hamilton Donnell
Annie Payson Call
Annie Roe Carr
Annonaymous
Anton Chekhov
Archibald Lee Fletcher
Arnold Bennett
Arthur C. Benson
Arthur Conan Doyle
Arthur M. Winfield
Arthur Ransome
Arthur Schnitzler
Arthur Train
Atticus
B.H. Baden-Powell
B. M. Bower
B. C. Chatterjee
Baroness Emmuska Orczy
Baroness Orczy
Basil King
Bayard Taylor
Ben Macomber
Bertha Muzzy Bower
Bjornstjerne Bjornson

Booth Tarkington
Boyd Cable
Bram Stoker
C. Collodi
C. E. Orr
C. M. Ingleby
Carolyn Wells
Catherine Parr Traill
Charles A. Eastman
Charles Amory Beach
Charles Dickens
Charles Dudley Warner
Charles Farrar Browne
Charles Ives
Charles Kingsley
Charles Klein
Charles Hanson Towne
Charles Lathrop Pack
Charles Romyn Dake
Charles Whibley
Charles Willing Beale
Charlotte M. Braeme
Charlotte M. Yonge
Charlotte Perkins Stetson
Clair W. Hayes
Clarence Day Jr.
Clarence E. Mulford
Clemence Housman
Confucius
Coningsby Dawson
Cornelis DeWitt Wilcox
Cyril Burleigh
D. H. Lawrence
Daniel Defoe
David Garnett
Dinah Craik
Don Carlos Janes
Donald Keyhoe
Dorothy Kilner
Dougan Clark
Douglas Fairbanks
E. Nesbit
E. P. Roe
E. Phillips Oppenheim
E. S. Brooks
Earl Barnes
Edgar Rice Burroughs
Edith Van Dyne
Edith Wharton

Edward Everett Hale
Edward J. O'Biren
Edward S. Ellis
Edwin L. Arnold
Eleanor Atkins
Eleanor Hallowell Abbott
Eliot Gregory
Elizabeth Gaskell
Elizabeth McCracken
Elizabeth Von Arnim
Ellem Key
Emerson Hough
Emilie F. Carlen
Emily Bronte
Emily Dickinson
Enid Bagnold
Enilor Macartney Lane
Erasmus W. Jones
Ernie Howard Pie
Ethel May Dell
Ethel Turner
Ethel Watts Mumford
Eugene Sue
Eugenie Foa
Eugene Wood
Eustace Hale Ball
Evelyn Everett-green
Everard Cotes
F. H. Cheley
F. J. Cross
F. Marion Crawford
Fannie E. Newberry
Federick Austin Ogg
Ferdinand Ossendowski
Fergus Hume
Florence A. Kilpatrick
Fremont B. Deering
Francis Bacon
Francis Darwin
Frances Hodgson Burnett
Frances Parkinson Keyes
Frank Gee Patchin
Frank Harris
Frank Jewett Mather
Frank L. Packard
Frank V. Webster
Frederic Stewart Isham
Frederick Trevor Hill
Frederick Winslow Taylor

Friedrich Kerst
Friedrich Nietzsche
Fyodor Dostoyevsky
G.A. Henty
G.K. Chesterton
Gabrielle E. Jackson
Garrett P. Serviss
Gaston Leroux
George A. Warren
George Ade
Geroge Bernard Shaw
George Cary Eggleston
George Durston
George Ebers
George Eliot
George Gissing
George MacDonald
George Meredith
George Orwell
George Sylvester Viereck
George Tucker
George W. Cable
George Wharton James
Gertrude Atherton
Gordon Casserly
Grace E. King
Grace Gallatin
Grace Greenwood
Grant Allen
Guillermo A. Sherwell
Gulielma Zollinger
Gustav Flaubert
H. A. Cody
H. B. Irving
H. C. Bailey
H. G. Wells
H. H. Munro
H. Irving Hancock
H. R. Naylor
H. Rider Haggard
H. W. C. Davis
Haldeman Julius
Hall Caine
Hamilton Wright Mabie
Hans Christian Andersen
Harold Avery
Harold McGrath
Harriet Beecher Stowe
Harry Castlemon
Harry Coghill
Harry Houidini

Hayden Carruth
Helent Hunt Jackson
Helen Nicolay
Hendrik Conscience
Hendy David Thoreau
Henri Barbusse
Henrik Ibsen
Henry Adams
Henry Ford
Henry Frost
Henry James
Henry Jones Ford
Henry Seton Merriman
Henry W Longfellow
Herbert A. Giles
Herbert Carter
Herbert N. Casson
Herman Hesse
Hildegard G. Frey
Homer
Honore De Balzac
Horace B. Day
Horace Walpole
Horatio Alger Jr.
Howard Pyle
Howard R. Garis
Hugh Lofting
Hugh Walpole
Humphry Ward
Ian Maclaren
Inez Haynes Gillmore
Irving Bacheller
Isabel Cecilia Williams
Isabel Hornibrook
Israel Abrahams
Ivan Turgenev
J. G.Austin
J. Henri Fabre
J. M. Barrie
J. M. Walsh
J. Macdonald Oxley
J. R. Miller
J. S. Fletcher
J. S. Knowles
J. Storer Clouston
J. W. Duffield
Jack London
Jacob Abbott
James Allen
James Andrews
James Baldwin

James Branch Cabell
James DeMille
James Joyce
James Lane Allen
James Lane Allen
James Oliver Curwood
James Oppenheim
James Otis
James R. Driscoll
Jane Abbott
Jane Austen
Jane L. Stewart
Janet Aldridge
Jens Peter Jacobsen
Jerome K. Jerome
Jessie Graham Flower
John Buchan
John Burroughs
John Cournos
John F. Kennedy
John Gay
John Glasworthy
John Habberton
John Joy Bell
John Kendrick Bangs
John Milton
John Philip Sousa
John Taintor Foote
Jonas Lauritz Idemil Lie
Jonathan Swift
Joseph A. Altsheler
Joseph Carey
Joseph Conrad
Joseph E. Badger Jr
Joseph Hergesheimer
Joseph Jacobs
Jules Vernes
Julian Hawthrone
Julie A Lippmann
Justin Huntly McCarthy
Kakuzo Okakura
Karle Wilson Baker
Kate Chopin
Kenneth Grahame
Kenneth McGaffey
Kate Langley Bosher
Kate Langley Bosher
Katherine Cecil Thurston
Katherine Stokes
L. A. Abbot
L. T. Meade

L. Frank Baum
Latta Griswold
Laura Dent Crane
Laura Lee Hope
Laurence Housman
Lawrence Beasley
Leo Tolstoy
Leonid Andreyev
Lewis Carroll
Lewis Sperry Chafer
Lilian Bell
Lloyd Osbourne
Louis Hughes
Louis Joseph Vance
Louis Tracy
Louisa May Alcott
Lucy Fitch Perkins
Lucy Maud Montgomery
Luther Benson
Lydia Miller Middleton
Lyndon Orr
M. Corvus
M. H. Adams
Margaret E. Sangster
Margret Howth
Margaret Vandercook
Margaret W. Hungerford
Margret Penrose
Maria Edgeworth
Maria Thompson Daviess
Mariano Azuela
Marion Polk Angellotti
Mark Overton
Mark Twain
Mary Austin
Mary Catherine Crowley
Mary Cole
Mary Hastings Bradley
Mary Roberts Rinehart
Mary Rowlandson
M. Wollstonecraft Shelley
Maud Lindsay
Max Beerbohm
Myra Kelly
Nathaniel Hawthrone
Nicolo Machiavelli
O. F. Walton
Oscar Wilde
Owen Johnson
P.G. Wodehouse
Paul and Mabel Thorne

Paul G. Tomlinson
Paul Severing
Percy Brebner
Percy Keese Fitzhugh
Peter B. Kyne
Plato
Quincy Allen
R. Derby Holmes
R. L. Stevenson
R. S. Ball
Rabindranath Tagore
Rahul Alvares
Ralph Bonehill
Ralph Henry Barbour
Ralph Victor
Ralph Waldo Emmerson
Rene Descartes
Ray Cummings
Rex Beach
Rex E. Beach
Richard Harding Davis
Richard Jefferies
Richard Le Gallienne
Robert Barr
Robert Frost
Robert Gordon Anderson
Robert L. Drake
Robert Lansing
Robert Lynd
Robert Michael Ballantyne
Robert W. Chambers
Rosa Nouchette Carey
Rudyard Kipling
Saint Augustine
Samuel B. Allison
Samuel Hopkins Adams
Sarah Bernhardt
Sarah C. Hallowell
Selma Lagerlof
Sherwood Anderson
Sigmund Freud
Standish O'Grady
Stanley Weyman
Stella Benson
Stella M. Francis
Stephen Crane
Stewart Edward White
Stijn Streuvels
Swami Abhedananda
Swami Parmananda
T. S. Ackland

T. S. Arthur
The Princess Der Ling
Thomas A. Janvier
Thomas A Kempis
Thomas Anderton
Thomas Bailey Aldrich
Thomas Bulfinch
Thomas De Quincey
Thomas Dixon
Thomas H. Huxley
Thomas Hardy
Thomas More
Thornton W. Burgess
U. S. Grant
Upton Sinclair
Valentine Williams
Various Authors
Vaughan Kester
Victor Appleton
Victor G. Durham
Victoria Cross
Virginia Woolf
Wadsworth Camp
Walter Camp
Walter Scott
Washington Irving
Wilbur Lawton
Wilkie Collins
Willa Cather
Willard F. Baker
William Dean Howells
William le Queux
W. Makepeace Thackeray
William W. Walter
William Shakespeare
Winston Churchill
Yei Theodora Ozaki
Yogi Ramacharaka
Young E. Allison
Zane Grey

www.ingramcontent.com/pod-product-compliance
Lightning Source LLC
Chambersburg PA
CBHW051837170626
46807CB00003B/1233